ADVANCE PRAISE FOR
Intertwined

"*Intertwined,* this story of a mother's hope, dedication, endurance, and strength, broke my heart in all the right ways. Kathleen English Cadmus has written a triumphant memoir."
—LEE MARTIN, author of *From Our House* and *The Bright Forever*

"A testament to a mother's love…At its heart, *Intertwined* is about resiliency and hope, about refusing to stop loving in the face of unthinkable loss and, finally, learning when it's time to let go. *Intertwined* is a must-read, full of grace."
—KATE HOPPER, author of *Ready for Air* and *Use Your Words: A Writer's Guide for Mothers*

"A heartfelt, brave, raw, yet hopeful journey of a mother's loss and unconditional love. Its honest look into grief and parenting a child with bipolar disorder will transfix and inspire."
—SHANNON HUDSON JOHNSON, Psy.D., clinical psychologist

"Nothing less than a new myth of who we are becoming: the multiethnic, transnational American family. Well done!"
—THOMAS LARSON, author of *The Memoir and the Memoirist, The Saddest Music Ever Written,* and *The Sanctuary of Illness*

"I highly recommend this book for everyone who has negotiated the journey of a devastating loss."
—CHRISTINE BOWERS, M.D., board-certified psychiatrist

"*Intertwined* contains many stories: a mother's agony at the death of a son, her joy in adopting a daughter from South Korea, her pursuit of this daughter who ran away from home, her daughter's reunion with her birth family, and the reconciliation of two mothers of the same child. What unifies these gripping, intertwined tales is the central paradox of parents and children, that 'running away' from those we love can eventually become 'running toward.' "

—STEVEN HARVEY, author of *The Book of Knowledge and Wonder* and senior editor at River Teeth Journal

"It has been a long time since I have started reading a book and was unable to put it down. *Intertwined* by Kathleen Cadmus provided me the opportunity to re-experience a 'guilty pleasure' I have not had for decades…. Not many of us have the courage to shine a bright light on our deepest sorrows and fears, nor the grit to examine them so closely. The wholeness achieved by such agonizing—but ultimately healing—processes is what being human is all about."

—JEANNE CLEMENT, APRN, PMHCNS, professor emeritus, The Ohio State University

Intertwined

A MOTHER'S MEMOIR

Kathleen English Cadmus

The lyrics to "Brother" have been printed with permission
from Dog Ear Music.

Cover and book design by Mark Sullivan

ISBN 978-0-9997422-3-5 (paperback)
ISBN 978-0-9997422-4-2 (e-book)

LIBRARY OF CONGRESS CATALOGING-IN-PUBLICATION DATA
Names: Cadmus, Kathleen English, author.
Title: Intertwined : a mother's memoir / by Kathleen English Cadmus.
Description: Georgetown, Ohio : KiCam Projects, [2018].
Identifiers: LCCN 2018057784 (print) | LCCN 2019006086 (ebook) |
ISBN 9780999742242 (ebook) | ISBN 9780999742235 (paperback) |
ISBN 9780999742242
(ebook)
Subjects: LCSH: Cadmus, Kathleen English. | Manic-depressive illness in
adolescence—Patients—United States—Biography. |
Children—Death—Biography. | Parent and child—United States. |
Parenting.
Classification: LCC RJ506.D4 (ebook) | LCC RJ506.D4 C33 2018 (print)
| DDC
616.89/50092 [B] —dc23
LC record available at https://lccn.loc.gov/2018057784

Printed in the United States of America

Published by KiCam Projects

www.KiCamProjects.com

for Shawn

∞

You've been gone for so many years
It makes me wonder what I did with
all my fears.
I still can feel you here.

Everything that I push away is me
asking you to stay 'cause
I can still feel you
running next to me.

I can still feel you running next to me
watching the clouds
breathe.

~ Peter English, *Brother*

TABLE OF CONTENTS

PART ONE

∞

Love recognizes no barriers. It jumps hurdles, leaps fences, penetrates walls to arrive at its destination full of hope.

~ Maya Angelou

You collapse against the closed door of your home, gasping for breath. Laughter escapes from deep in your throat as you wipe away your tears.

You just hired a bounty hunter.

You. A freaking bounty hunter!

An energizing sense of power and determination surges through you.

Your sixteen-year-old daughter is missing.

Laura.

Gone.

Where is she? What is she doing? Will you ever see her again...alive?

You are beside yourself. You have been that way for the ten days she's been gone. It isn't the first time Laura has disappeared from your sight, but this time is different. An autumn night with temperatures falling, clothes on her back befitting a hot summer day, medications left behind in her bathroom cabinet, and her cell phone left behind on the kitchen table all intensify your panic.

You are inflamed by the lack of results from the local police to find your daughter.

But it is the memories of the past two years that bore into your heart and infuse you with fear. Memories of watching her transition from happy, social, school-loving, and overachieving to isolative, sulky, unpredictable, and unmotivated; of retrieving her from the State Highway Patrol after they stopped her for driving eighty-five miles per hour after a three-day absence from home; of sitting next to her on the adolescent psychiatric unit while meeting with hospital staff, discussing her treatment, her depression palpable; of enduring the sleepless nights this past summer during the twenty-one days she was missing before finally being found by police, alone on the dark streets of East Cleveland.

The horror of those memories pushes you to do everything you can to find her.

So, you cash out your 401(k) and hire Stewart Wackman as your personal bounty hunter.

As you sit at your kitchen table with Stewart, sorting through photos of Laura, you feel a glimmer of hope. Hope that this muscular, six-foot-five African-American male can track down your diminutive, four-foot-ten Korean-American daughter. She might finally be found. Brought home to you again.

You refuse to let the gripping fear of never seeing your daughter again take hold. You close your eyes and breathe deeply. Then opening your eyes, you tell Stewart about the last time you saw Laura.

Your last glimpse: Laura, happily running up the family room stairs, heading to bed, her black hair swaying across her back, her bare feet skimming the carpet, the muscles of her short calves flexing with each step.

CHAPTER ONE

Beginnings, February 27, 1985

*Anyone who ever wondered how much they could love
a child who did not spring from their own loins, know
this: it is the same. The feeling of love is so profound, it's
incredible and surprising.*

~ Nia Vardalos, *Instant Mom*

It was fifteen years earlier when I had waited for my first glimpse
of Laura.

I stood next to Helen, my assigned airport guide, and peered
into the snowy February sky, scanning the runway at Chicago's
O'Hare International Airport. My heart pounded in my chest. It
was like being in labor without the contractions and the pushing
and the panting. Helen was my labor nurse. I started taking deep
breaths, in through my nose, out through my mouth, attempting
to keep my breathing even. I glued my eyes to a snow cloud in
the sky, using it as a focal point. I had given birth to three babies
via natural childbirth, *sans* drugs. Yet as I waited at the airport,
I thought how helpful it would be to have something to quiet
my pounding heart. Anything to tame the butterflies causing my
gut to cramp. I silently prayed, "Please bring her safely to me."
Then, remembering there were other expectant parents around
me—ten or twelve of us waiting for our Korean-born children—
and not wanting to be selfish, I added, "Keep all those children
safe and bring them to their forever homes."

"One parent per adoptee," is what Helen had told Will,
Ryan, and me when we met shortly after arriving at O'Hare.

She was referring to the area of the airport where one of us would wait for the plane. Will and I agreed it should be me, the mom, rather than him, the dad, to first meet our daughter. I had been relieved when our adoption agency told us there would be someone assigned to help us navigate the airport. Helen, light-haired and appearing to be in her late thirties, close to my age, was competent and organized. I don't know what her job description entailed, but the sparkle in her eyes and the smile on her face led me to think she was just as thrilled as I was to be meeting our daughter.

Just after meeting us, Helen led us to an observation area. She leaned in slightly toward Ryan, touching his arm and pointing to Customs below, saying, "You and your dad can watch your mom as she comes through those doors with your new sister." As Helen and I walked away, I turned my head and waved at Ryan. Chubby-cheeked and fair, he suddenly appeared younger to me than his ten years. He smiled and waved back.

As I waited, I engaged in small talk with those around me. Adoption small talk: "Are you getting a son or a daughter?" and "Where do you live?" and "Do you have other children?" We exchanged nervous smiles with one another, like graduates standing in line waiting for their diplomas and the turn of their tassels. We expectant parents had all earned this moment and we knew our lives were about to change.

My prayers were intermittently interrupted with intrusive doubts. *Would I know her?* Certainly she would have grown. The pictures sent to us had been taken when she was nine months old. Big eyes, skinny legs, and just enough hair to stick straight up on her head. Now she would be fourteen months old, already having celebrated her first birthday. *Would she like me?* Babies usually did like me. I had been known to soothe even the most fretful child. *What if she cries? What if she becomes inconsolable in my arms?*

I stood as close to the window as possible, sometimes on tiptoes to stretch my not-quite-five-foot-two frame. Then I saw the outline of a silver bullet. First the nose, then the wings, turning and slowly navigating its way along the runway through the gray mist toward the gate.

"There's our plane," Helen said smiling. "She's here." The butterflies in my stomach became little sparks traveling up my body, giving me goose bumps and stinging my eyes. This was really happening. We stood and waited as travelers filed out from the plane, dragging luggage and belongings and sometimes children of their own. Most passengers had dark hair and East Asian eyes and spoke Korean words I did not understand. Finally, Helen turned to me and smiled. "It's okay now. Only the babies and escorts are left on the plane. Let's go find your daughter."

I followed Helen past the gate, through the tunnel, and onto the plane. A few feet down on the left side of the aisle, my eyes came to rest on a child dwarfed by the high back of the airplane seat. In my memory, she is the only one I saw. This little child—*my* child—dressed in bright red from head to toe, sitting all alone as though she had flown here all by herself in that big plane. Her face was round, much rounder than in the photos—now stuck with magnets on my refrigerator door—sent to me from the adoption agency. But the eyes. Those unforgettable eyes. Her solemn, eyes-straight-ahead gaze. I knew it was her. The pinkness of her face was accentuated by her red clothing. Her cheeks were flushed. Her black hair, grown longer than in the photographs, was dark and silky against her face.

I picked her up and hugged her. I could feel the hard, rapid pulsing of her heart through her heavy clothing. I already knew she had a heart defect, yet I was shocked that I could feel it. It took my breath away. Each beat was a pulsating reminder that Laura came with a risk, a high probability of heart surgery in her future.

She was quiet and calm. As she stared at me, I wished she could tell me what she was thinking, what she was feeling. There were fourteen months of life's happenings stored in her mind and heart that I knew nothing about. An uncontrollable smile spread across my face. I kissed her soft, round cheek.

"Hi, Sweetie," I whispered.

We kept our eyes on each other as we exited the plane. I carried her directly to the bathroom for a diaper change. Everything she brought with her from her homeland was on her body. She wore a thick, red, hooded jacket that snapped up the front and matching fleece pants with elastic at the feet and waist. Animal ears decorated the hood of her jacket with smaller versions attached to her red cloth shoes, which she wore over thick, brown socks. Under her jacket and pants, she wore pale gold, footed pajamas. Small Olympic figures performing their summer sports covered the pajama arms and legs, back and front, a reminder that Seoul was preparing for the 1988 Summer Olympic Games.

I took the small bottle of Johnson's baby lotion from my purse and rubbed the lotion on her legs, arms, face, and neck. I inhaled the familiar scent, which carried memories of my three little boys. It took me back to the early months of each child's life, when I would bathe them, rub lotion on their skin, and feel their softness against me, claiming them as my own. I picked her up and held her close. Laura clasped my sweater with one small hand and made a tight fist around my fingers with the other.

We journeyed through Customs, me with a smile I could not erase, and Laura with her solemn gaze focused on me. After Laura's passport had been stamped by Customs, I glanced up and saw Will and Ryan waving at us from the observation area. Will took a picture from above, Laura's round cheeks pressing against mine, strands of her black hair resting against my longer, dark brown hair. Then, with Ryan in tow, Will headed toward us. Laura's face showed no emotion as she was passed to Will and then to Ryan, turning her gaze from them to me. She sat still as a doll while Helen snapped more photos.

Our drive to Chicago had begun the day before. Snow had fallen in big, fat flakes, piling up quickly on the roads and lengthening a drive that would have taken six hours in good weather. We had stayed the night in a hotel close to the airport in order to meet Laura's early-morning flight. I had fretted about the snow as it piled up, fearing it would prevent us from reaching the airport. I had imagined her plane, unable to land in a blizzard, turning and flying back to South Korea, my arms reaching out— but never far enough to touch my waiting child.

With Laura now safely in my arms, we were ready to go home. We were on the road back to Ohio by early afternoon. Laura didn't cry at all on the way home. She tilted her head and stared motionlessly at Ryan, as one might stare at a blue goose if it waddled over and sat beside you on a park bench. She rarely took her eyes off him. Ryan was fair-skinned with blue eyes and light hair that turned almost white in the summer. We soon realized she had probably never seen anyone in Korea who looked quite like Ryan.

Her new brother made silly faces and noises to entertain her. It was four hours into the trip before we heard her first sounds made on American soil. She started to giggle, revealing deep dimples high on her cheeks.

Our fifteen-year-old son, Pete, who didn't like crowds and airports, was not with us, having opted to not miss school or soccer practice. He waited at home with my mother, a widow since my college years. She had made the two-hour drive from her home to ours the day before. My Mom and Pete would be our welcome-home party of two.

Chapter Two

Shawn, March 19, 1983

I will never forget the moment your heart stopped and mine kept beating.

~ Angela Miller

Shawn, our middle son, had been the catalyst for the adoption of Laura. Shawn and the events that had taken place the day he left for his first Boy Scout campout.

It was a Saturday. Everyone in our family had plans for the day. We were a happy family of five—Will, our three boys (thirteen-year-old Pete, eleven-year-old Shawn, eight-year-old Ryan), and I. Will and I had married young, finished college, worked hard, and played by the rules. We knew life had been good to us and assumed it would stay that way.

Our home was always full of boys. Shawn was the magnet that drew most of them in: Jay, Matt, Steve, Mark, Danny, Chad. But Jay was the friend who was with Shawn the most, having earned the label *best friend* in the second grade. Eating and chatting, arms punctuating words, bodies fidgeting—common scenes at our kitchen table. Their friendship had been further defined in a school assignment in which students were asked to think about their family and friends.

Who can you think of that is most like you?

Shawn's answer: *"My friend, Jay Miller, because we are the same height, the same weight, and both like the same sports. We also like the same video games."* Shawn focused on what they shared and saw only how they were similar.

They also shared the same enthusiasm for the upcoming weekend Boy Scout camping trip. I watched and listened as they ate breakfast in the pre-dawn hours of that crisp March morning, tousled blond hair next to a thick, dark Afro; Shawn's fair, freckled skin contrasting with Jay's dark, smooth arms; bright, sky-blue eyes meeting warm, earthy brown ones.

Shawn opened his mouth and took a breath to talk, his arm suspended midway between his lips and his oversized spoonful of Cheerios. "Awesome! Today's going to be just awesome, that's what I think."

Will had thought Shawn too busy to add scouting to his schedule. Shawn was undeniably a very busy boy: a member of two indoor soccer teams, president of his class, a drum student, and an after-school newspaper carrier. Although I did not share Will's concern, it did prompt me to question Shawn.

"Don't you think you need to slow down?" I asked him one evening after he fell asleep while doing his homework. "You have the rest of your life to do all this new stuff."

"Good, Mom, I'm good." His response, infused with a smile partially swallowed by a yawn, assured me he had it all under control. I lacked immunity from Shawn's contagious enthusiasm. It infected me. I was the parent who had supported his interest in joining the Scouts.

Shawn and I said our *love you*s at the front door that Saturday morning. As I was growing up, my family hadn't expressed much verbal affection. After my father died suddenly when I was in college, I felt compelled to change. I verbalized *love* whenever I could. It became a ritual, having a rhythm of its own, as necessary as the dependable beating of a heart.

"Love you, Shawn," I said as he headed out the door, backpack on his back.

"Love you too, Mom." Shawn's words came packaged with a grin and a wraparound two-armed hug, something he had recently added as his own signature goodbye.

❧

Eight hours later, I was summoned from the home of my friend, with whom I'd spent the day shopping and chatting.

"Just come home! Now!" Will insisted on the phone.

I heard the news of Shawn's accident as I stood in our entryway, door wide open. I could feel the breeze at my back. Felt like spring.

"Shawn fell," Will said. "Hit his head."

His voice strained, his words sputtering out from his dry, tight throat as he told me our fearless, nature-loving son had fallen.

"Rescuers rappelled down," he explained while I stared at my family standing like statues around me. *What happened to their faces? Why was everyone wearing masks? Pale masks with glazed eyes and wet cheeks. Will. Pete. Ryan. Wearing masks.*

"They tried…"

"They couldn't…"

Slowly I began to understand Will's words.

Shawn had plummeted—seventy feet—into a ravine. He and Jay were sitting on the edge of a cliff, kicking stones over the edge. Shawn stood up. His foot slipped and caught a tree root, flipping him upside down.

And seconds later, Shawn's head smashed into a slate-bottomed ravine. His right eye was destroyed. His beautiful, perfect blue eye. Shawn landed so deep into the ravine, it took rescuers an hour to reach him.

Will's words faded away.

All I could hear was a piercing, animal-like cry...a wail, coming from somewhere dark and deep.

My chest hurt. I was cold. So cold.

Why was it so hard to breathe?

That sound. What was that sound?

Oh...no.

That sound.

It was coming from me.

∞

That night, lying in bed, I could see my son's life in review. Not only the eleven-year-old boy he was that morning, but the fat-cheeked infant he had once been as he slept in my arms. The toddler in nursery school, grabbing the thick curls of a little boy whose teeth were embedded in his arm, Shawn's firm grip pulling those curls in quiet determination. And the adventurous preschooler, pedaling hard on his mini-wheel, trying to keep up with Pete on his big-wheel.

My eyes opened; my eyes closed. I saw his wide-faced grin. Lips pressed together, cheeks squeezed upward into the crinkles of his eyes. That grin, plastered on his three-year-old face as he posed proudly for a photo while sitting in an over-sized yellow rocker, arms wrapped securely around the wiggly baby brother, Ryan, on his lap. His grin showing pure joy when he made his first soccer goal...and rolling in the grass, laughing and laughing with his friends...and giving our golden retriever, Bridgette, a wrap-around hug, draping his body against her back, Shawn's face pressed against her soft muzzle, his sun-streaked hair blending with her golden fur.

My face. Hot and wet. Nose stuffy. Too tired to move. I

curled up into the fetal position near the edge of my bed.

Shawn grinned at me, swinging his backpack to his shoulder as he headed out the door.

"Love you, Mom."

I licked the salty wetness from my lips.

CHAPTER THREE

Life after Death

I find it impossible to let a friend or relative go into that country of no return.

Disbelief becomes my close companion and anger follows in its wake.

I answer the heroic question, "Death, where is thy sting?" with

"It is here in my heart and mind and memories."

~ Maya Angelou, *Wouldn't Take Nothing for My Journey Now*

In the early days of our grief, Will and I took turns supporting and leaning on each other. The day following Shawn's accident, after Will shook his head and turned away from the newspaper reporter in our home, I fielded the intrusive questions for both of us.

"What have you learned about how the accident happened? Have you talked with the Scout leaders? What did he like to do with his brothers? Did he take care of your dog?" I answered the reporter's questions while I sat on our living room sofa and looked out our bay window at the grassy hill where our kids loved to play. Small spring leaves on the trees along the side of the hill made shadows on the greening grass. No children now. I denied her request for a photo of our family holding Shawn's picture. "Let's put your dog in the photo too," she had eagerly suggested.

"Uh, no...don't think so," I told her as I eyed our golden retriever lying on her belly, paws tucked under her jaw, ears draped on the floor; her big brown eyes rolling from me to the reporter and back to me again. Bridgette wanted no part of it. Smart dog. I pictured a pathetic and incomplete family photo, bleeding newspaper ink onto the cold, damp stoops of the neighborhood homes as it delivered our tragic news. To be fair, the reporter was soft-spoken and polite. But what did she know about grief, anyway? She accepted my offer of Shawn's recent class picture as a compromising gesture.

When Will and I later walked hand in hand through the doors of the funeral home, we were matching bookends of confusion and shock. The man who greeted us was unusually tall and thin, appearing as if he had just emerged from being closed up flat in a Murphy bed. I guessed him to be close to my age, in his mid to late thirties. Mr. "Murphy" had the aura of someone in a consistent state of deep meditation, speaking in a voice just a few decibels above a whisper. Why the whisper? Did he fear awakening the dead?

I found Mr. Murphy's presence irritating, but not as obnoxious as the smell that permeated the room, a thick, flowery mixture of carnations, roses, and other funeral bouquets. The smells alone were enough to submerge someone into eternal sleep. I wanted the smell of snickerdoodles. Shawn loved to make snickerdoodles. Baking them was often his after-school project—dough half-eaten, two dozen cookies cooling from the four-dozen-cookie recipe when I would arrive home from work. I wanted the scent of cinnamon. I wanted the taste of that sweet dough. I wanted the sounds of boisterous children ringing in my ears.

As I stood in the room with empty caskets and vaults, I remembered my visits as a child to the home of a friend who grew up in her family's funeral home. She would lead me into her home through the basement door, which forced us to pass through the room where caskets were stored. I would take my shoes off and run tiptoe, as quietly and as quickly as I could, to reach the doorway leading to the safety of her bedroom. Now, standing with Will and Mr. Murphy in the casket room, I wanted to be ten years old again, to take my shoes off and run as fast as I could to safety.

While my throat ached with tightness and my insides felt shaky, Will remained steady enough to take charge. I was grateful. As I stood by his side, he communicated calmly with Mr. Murphy, taming his own inner chaos by chewing on his bottom lip. He filled out forms, handled the details of the death certificate, and orchestrated the logistics of the calling hours and burial.

Shawn was patched up for calling hours, his destroyed right eye covered and less visible to mourners as they approached his left side, his fractured legs hidden under a soft, blue quilt. The line of grievers went out the door, down the steps, and up the street. At Pete's insistence (*"Please, Mom, don't put him in a suit. He'd hate it."*), Shawn wore a red plaid shirt and blue cords and was sock-footed. His treasured soccer shoes were placed by his feet, the teddy bear he still slept with tucked close by his side. Will and I stood together at the calling hours with Pete and Ryan, next to Shawn with his hidden broken bones, patched-up eye, and silent heart.

I had resisted this grieving ritual, but I began to feel like I was being useful. I was at the core of a vigilance committee, protecting and shielding Shawn from any more harm. We were all together again. Our family. A small wave of comfort came over me as I kept a watchful eye on him, giving my sorrow a temporary respite. So painful to leave that night and go home without him, leaving him alone.

Thursday evening, we held a memorial service at the United Methodist Church where Shawn had been baptized as an infant and nurtured as a child. Will and I wanted a real celebration, a safe place where Pete and Ryan could share more about who their brother was, where Shawn's friends could know how important they were in our lives, and to have the world stand still for a brief period of time to honor Shawn. Our church was packed full with friends, classmates, and neighbors, leaving me in awe at how many people Shawn's life had touched.

Will and I had selected music, readings, and poems that we wanted at the memorial. But it was the words of others that helped soothe me. Shawn's brief life was important to many. His life brought joy to people I had never met. Others knew him as sweet, loving, fun, and kind. Not just his mom.

"When I received the news of Shawn's death, I cried and grieved as though I had lost one of my own children. I felt tremendous sorrow and hurt, and cheated by this loss," lamented his sixth-grade teacher, Mr. Wilson.

And from his young friends:

"I feel a part of me is gone…"

"Shawn is the most kindest and helpful person in the world…"

"…and I'll never forget him."

"I was here for one year and he would never talk about me like the other kids. He was nice to me. We miss him very much."

"…he will always be deep in my heart."

"Shawn was my best friend. I will always remember him as long as I live."

And another child's words of comfort: *"P.S. I'm sure God is taking good care of him."*

On Friday, our journey to the cemetery began at the funeral home on High Street, passing the Methodist church where Will had dropped off Shawn for the early-morning camping departure, giving his son his last hug. The procession slowly picked up speed, passing the street corner where our family had often watched and, on occasion, had marched in the annual Memorial Day parade, and the Dairy Queen where our boys would take their paper route earnings on a hot summer day. We stopped at a traffic light, our home up the street to the right, a field where many soccer wins had been celebrated to the left. I closed my eyes, still seeing the passing of Shawn's childhood landmarks, and finally feeling the shift in gears as we merged onto the highway and settled into freeway speed for the three-hour drive to the city where Will and I had grown up, where our parents still lived, and where my father had been buried fifteen years earlier.

I stood with Will at the top of a hill and watched as strong hands, grasping the cold handles of the casket, moved Shawn to the open space where my father and my son would lie side by side.

Chapter Four

Each in Our Own Way

As one parent said, "My child's gone; I'm still here. My job is to figure out my purpose now."
~ Elaine Stillwell, *The Death of a Child: Reflections for Grieving Parents*

As we drove out of the cemetery toward home, I could feel Will's vulnerability. He had appeared organized and calm while managing the events of the calling hours and funeral, but once those tasks were taken care of, he looked for other ways to be in control. Friends, coworkers, and family saw Will's calm, quiet, and seemingly accepting demeanor. But *I* felt the irritability, anger, and control that began to dominate Will's moods.

Will insisted we still take a modified form of the vacation he had planned before Shawn's accident, a trip to Florida scheduled to begin the day after our son's burial. The original plan was for Will and our three boys to take the week of spring break and visit his parents in Florida. I would stay home and continue to work. But then Shawn was gone, and Will's parents had made a hasty trip back to Ohio for the funeral. The trip became a *family* trip with Will, Pete, Ryan, me, and Will's parents. We would stay a week, and then his parents would pack up their winter place in Florida and return with us to their home in Ohio. The trip was torture for me. The shortest route from Ohio to Florida went through mountains. Driving through the mountains, I kept seeing Shawn, then me, falling down and crashing head first onto rock. In Florida, I found myself telling a stunned pharmacist at a little pharmacy on the beach my "story" of the past week, filling his head with all the horrors while I waited for a prescription for an anxiety med to be filled. I was in a perpetual hypervigilant state. I worried constantly about Pete and Ryan, fearing they might fall into the ocean or disappear during the night. I couldn't bear to have Pete or Ryan out of my sight, even when I closed my eyes to sleep.

A controlled anger dominated Will's mood and masked his grieving. While we were in Florida and often during the following weeks, he was in a frenzy, focusing on the details and facts of Shawn's accident. He coped with his confused feelings by investigating how and why his son had died. He tried to tackle the question of *how could the most athletic kid in the group of seven Scouts have fallen to his death while accompanied by five responsible adults?* A question too painful for me to ponder.

Will did not release his tears but pushed them inward where they steamed and fueled his anger. But where can you put such anger? So much anger? Where can it go without becoming destructive when it blows into rage?

It seemed as if my tears would never end. I cried more than enough for both of us, which left me without the strength needed to deal with Will's simmering fury. I was drowning in my own sorrow. I felt as if my chest and gut had been scooped out. Left empty. A close friend suggested I go to Compassionate Friends, a support group for parents who have lost a child. "It will help you to be around others," she said. "You know, other parents like you." Meaning, of course, parents with dead children.

I asked Will to come with me. He declined. "You go if you want," hands on his hips, head bent down. Then, turning his weary, blue eyes toward me, he added, "There is no room on this earth big enough to contain all my anger. Go if you want."

I went to the meeting by myself. I opened the heavy door of the church, turned left as instructed, and entered a room packed with people. The room smelled of cigarette smoke and coffee. I stood there frozen in a sea of chatting, socializing, laughing people. A smiling, unshaven man, coffee cup in hand, approached me and lightly touched my arm. "Honey," he said in a husky smoker's voice, "I think you want the room down the hall. This is an AA meeting."

He led me to a small room in a corner of the building. Peering into the room, I could see chairs in a circle with eight to ten people present. Coffee, tea, and cookies had been placed on a small table. Boxes of tissues sat at attention throughout the room. For an instant, I wanted to join the happy group down the hall. They appeared to be fighting friendlier demons than the ones I was attempting to battle. But I turned and thanked the husky-voiced man, wondering how he knew this was where I belonged. Did I have "grieving mother, handle with care" stamped on my forehead?

The room was quieter, the voices softer than those in the other room. No one felt uncomfortable when I cried in this group. They just passed the tissues. I felt no burden of sympathy to endure. I learned the crazy things I found myself doing were not a sign I was losing my sanity. No one gasped when I talked about the day I left my cart in the grocery store aisle and fled, too overwhelmed by all the reminders of Shawn. The others in the group just nodded when I told them I had driven around the block three times one day because I wanted to look one more time at the little blond-haired boy walking to school, thinking maybe the next time he turned his head, it would be Shawn. He would say, "Hi, Mom!"

No, I wasn't crazy. I was grieving.

When I would awaken each morning during those first weeks after Shawn's death, I felt as if I were in the wrong place. It was an unfamiliar world where something was missing, almost as if I had lost a body part—an arm, an eye, a part of me. Pete and Ryan were my sole motivation to drag myself out of bed.

It was not just me who felt different. We all did, individually and as a family. We were unbalanced. I thought back to the summer months and our last family vacation in Michigan. So many of our family vacations had involved lakes or oceans. Sand and beaches. I replayed seeing our three boys, their hair bleached light by the summer sun, digging in the sand building tunnels or covering each other in mounds of sand or making castles and detailed sand structures. I didn't remember the moment when an ocean wave would come in and wash away whatever it was they were building, but surely it did. I only remembered the togetherness and the joy of those seemingly endless summer days. But suddenly, like a washed-away sand castle, our beautiful family we had built was gone. Swept away in a tidal wave of sudden grief.

∾

Will and I had been a couple, married three years, when the birth of Pete had made us a family. Two years later, Shawn was born. They quickly became not just brothers but best friends. By the time they reached the ages of almost fourteen and almost twelve, they shared a room, shared friends, and shared a love of the game of soccer. In their words, they were "best buds."

The January before Shawn's accident, Pete and Shawn became teammates on a competitive indoor soccer team. Since they were two years apart in school, the division for the team placement had always put them in different age groups. But for this team, even though Shawn was a sixth-grader, he was placed on the seventh- and eighth-grade team. In the weeks after Shawn's death, I clung to a photo of the two boys taken during the soccer season. They stand shoulder to shoulder in front of our fireplace. Both are grinning. Shawn, standing with his legs apart, right arm across Pete's shoulders, head held high, stretching up to Pete's taller frame. And Pete, body relaxed, arms slightly bent, his hands gripping the arms of a pair of crutches he had allowed his body to relax into. Pete had fractured his right ankle during the intensity of a game, having his foot stepped on by another player attempting to defend the ball. Pete's foot healed well enough by the end of the season to play in the final tournament, but the week before the tournament started, Shawn was gone. The soccer league dedicated the playoff game to Shawn and our team took first place. Pete chose not to play.

The photo is the last one taken of the two of them together. It makes me cry and feel joy at the same time. It is a happy photo. The kind of happy that gives me the illusion that if only I could listen more intently, I would hear their laughter once again.

I thought about an incident that had happened one afternoon when I was eight months pregnant with Ryan. Pete was five, Shawn was three, and I was resting during their naptime. My motherly instinct poked me with a sudden urge to check on my napping sons. Quietly I bare-footed across the carpeted hall and peered into their bedroom. The boys stood at the open, narrow, floor-to-ceiling window. The screen had been popped off. Pete stood behind Shawn, his hands on Shawn's shoulders. Shawn was clothed in red-and-blue Underoos, a miniature Superman wannabe, blue cape tied in a crooked bow below his chin. Both boys had their backs to me with their eyes focused on the grass outside, one story below.

"Stop!" I yelled. "Don't move! What are you doing?"

Pete turned, removing his hands from the shoulders of his more willing brother. The afternoon sun highlighted Pete's hair. His eyes seemed bigger, his pupils black dots in his steel-blue eyes. Quickly Pete whispered, "We wanted to see if we could fly."

Pete was the architect; Shawn was the action figure. Pete had the creative mind, Shawn the fearless courage. Already at that point, they had built a friendship and a relationship exclusive to the two of them. They understood each other's needs and strengths and they were loyal to one another.

Ryan was born less than a month after Pete and Shawn's aborted attempt at flying out their bedroom window. Ryan was the fairest of the three, affectionately called "the white tornado" by a friend in preschool. Ryan has always been my sweetest child. I'm not sure whether he was born that way or if he acquired his sweetness from being treated as the family prize by his brothers. It was easy for them to treat him kindly, for Ryan had a calm and trusting personality mixed with an innate abundance of imaginative thinking.

There were many times when we would laugh about what Ryan was seeing in his world. We were puzzled about the "cloud factory" Ryan insisted was located near our home, until he suddenly yelled, "Mom!" from the back seat of the car one sunny afternoon as we drove past the Busch brewery. "See, Mom, that's where the clouds are made!" he had gleefully explained. I glanced to my left, the musty, yeasty Cheez-It smell in my nostrils, and realized the source of Ryan's clouds was the brewery belching white puffs of smoke against a flawless, blue autumn sky. Then there was Ryan's request for me to play the "Pete-y-Shawn" song one more time in the car, after we had listened to "Tradition" from *Fiddler on the Roof* multiple times. We all heard "Tradition!" and Ryan would sing along "Pete-y-Shawn!" and make us all chuckle.

For Pete, losing his best friend and brother was life-shattering. His fear and anxiety blossomed. Sometimes he acted out his fears during his sleep. In the middle of a humid night in August, five months after Shawn's death, I was awakened by our doorbell and the whining of our dog. I hesitantly crept down the stairs and peered around to see the front door. Bridgette stood in the entranceway, tail wagging in gleeful anticipation at what was on the other side. I could see the side of Pete's face through the small window in our door. Opening the door, I found Pete, rocking from one foot to the other, clad only in his thin summer shorts.

"I think I fell out of bed," he calmly explained. When I realized Pete had popped out the screen of his bedroom window, stepped through its narrow opening, and landed feet-first, inches away from our air conditioning unit below, it felt like my heart was beating in my throat. Looking at Pete, unharmed, I chose to believe Pete had a guardian angel. *Could it be Shawn?*

Sleep studies confirmed he was sleepwalking and having panic attacks in his sleep. Therapy confirmed he needed more help with his grief than Will or I would be able to provide.

Ryan was eight when Shawn died. A few weeks after Shawn's death, Ryan was walked home by two of Shawn's sixth-grade classmates. "Ryan told us if we walked him home, we would get to see Shawn," one of the girls told me. "He said Shawn was coming back. Do you think Ryan is going to be okay?" she asked me, concerned.

I explained to her that being eight years old is a difficult time to lose a brother. "Eight-year-olds are stuck somewhere between reality and make-believe," I told her, falling short of revealing that I, too, entertained the fantasy that Shawn would be there one day when I walked in the door.

Shawn's adventurous, easygoing nature had been the bridge between Pete, our perfectionistic firstborn, and Ryan, our easy-to-please lastborn. The boys did not simply *miss* Shawn, they deeply grieved their brother's death.

∞

When Shawn died, I was working full time as an office nurse in the OB/GYN practice of Dr. Roger Hamer. Dr. Hamer had shown extraordinary compassion. Ryan and Shawn had attended the same elementary school and had walked to and from school together each day. But after Shawn had died, Ryan, then a second-grader, instead would attend an after-school program until I could pick him up after work. Dr. Hamer sensed my protectiveness about Ryan. Without my asking, he suggested I limit my time at his office to the hours Ryan would be in school.

"Get here when you can and leave when you need to pick up Ryan," he advised.

So that became my schedule for the remainder of the school year.

Will's anger over Shawn's death had surfaced quickly. His anger was visible in each muscle and fiber of his being, audible in the tone and timbre of his voice. In contrast, my anger lay deep and hidden, feeding my sadness, darkening my mood. But one steamy August day, five months after Shawn had died, it erupted unexpectedly. Two boys who had been with Shawn on the campout came to visit me, as many of Shawn's friends did. They were boys who had not been frequent visitors at our home, and it was the first time I had seen them since the memorial service. They wanted me to know how they had helped Shawn and that all of the boys had performed some life-saving task when they reached him after his fall into the ravine.

We all went for help. I started the CPR. I tried to stop the bleeding. I held his hand.

I listened quietly. I hugged them when they left, giving them both a T-shirt of Shawn's at their request. Then I went to my basement and picked up a child's wooden chair. I beat it against the wall and smashed it repeatedly on the floor while I wailed and screamed and cried. I had no inkling of what I was thinking and feeling. All I knew was I had to purge this horrible force that had welled up inside of me. This alien, ugly force. I beat that sweet, innocent little red chair until it lay in pieces, exorcised and pulverized into a pile of broken and splintered matchsticks on my basement floor.

After summer break and when autumn arrived, I returned to work full time, but my energy was low. The shortening of daylight hours exacerbated my dread of winter. I would have gladly hop-skipped over the Thanksgiving and Christmas holidays that year. The cold started early, turning the earth a dull brown and the sky a dirty gray. Was it really colder than usual? I don't know, but the cold managed to seep deeply into my bones. Shopping malls with cheap Christmas reds and greens, boisterous voices, and radios pumping out "Joy to the World," alternating with tales of poor Grandma who "Got Run Over by a Reindeer," only stirred the angry spot inside me.

Over the ensuing months, the empty sensation in my chest and gut did eventually start to become bearable. The laughter and joy and memories, like grains of sand, were still there. We had to reshape and rebuild, add a bridge or a new room, build a new sandcastle from the old. Time moved on, with days passing into months, and months passing the first anniversary of Shawn's death. Will and I went through our daily tasks and routines, me at Dr. Hamer's office and Will as a supervisor at Children Services. I remember feeling isolated and disconnected from him. I assumed he felt the same way about me. But neither one of us made a move to change things.

No matter where I went, the grief went with me. It had taken root inside me. I began to realize I needed to find meaning and a sense of purpose for Shawn's life that went beyond memorials planted in school yards, scholarships awarded to aid his still-living classmates, and attempts to identify someone we could hold accountable for our loss. More than that, I was grasping for a greater meaning and purpose in my own life. My life continued. My son's did not.

As another spring break came and went, I started to ruminate about having another child. I yearned to feel the softness of a little child's forehead on my lips, to smell the freshness of a toddler's skin after a bath. I wanted to once again sit in my wooden rocker with a small child asleep in my arms, breathing on my neck as we watched the night turn into the early morning light. I craved one more chance to do it again, to gather the sands of my life that had scattered in the storm of grief, and to rebuild.

CHAPTER FIVE

Being the Mom

Adoption is grief in reverse.
~ Jody Cantrell Dyer, The Eye of Adoption

Shawn had died two days before my thirty-eighth birthday, so I was still young enough to have another biological child. But I was interested in adoption. I felt a desire to make a difference in the life of a child who had already been born into this world.

I wanted to mother a motherless child.

I understand now that my desire to adopt a child had its beginning at the edge of a cliff in Hocking Hills. Shawn falling to his death screamed out the message of the fleeting years of my child's life, forcing me to face the impermanence of all my children's lives. My own life.

Are there right and wrong reasons for adoption? Probably. But, the *me* who pondered adoption felt passion and yearning and desire. Reasons enough for me. Adoption was a way to show Pete and Ryan that love does go on; it doesn't die with death. Love is permanent. And living life following Shawn's example was the best way to honor his life. Our Shawn did not live for yesterday. He grabbed the moments of his todays, always eager for tomorrow. Adoption was a commitment to tomorrow.

I believed if Shawn had been standing before me and I could have asked him, "What do you think about us adopting a child?" his answer, "Awesome, Mom. Awesome," would have come with a grin and his signature wraparound, two-armed hug.

One spring evening, more than a year after Shawn had died, Will and I were walking near our children's elementary school. An honorary scarlet maple tree, planted by Shawn's classmates, stood at the front of the school. One of us often would initiate such a walk with, "Let's go see how Shawn's tree is growing."

I brought up the subject of adoption. Again. For I had been dropping the subject into our conversations over the past few months.

"Remember how we looked into adoption shortly after Pete was born? We used to listen to a weekly ten-minute local TV segment on adoption when they would spotlight a needy child."

"'Tuesday's Child,' I think they called it," Will commented.

"Sounds right," I agreed. "We had no money back then. God, we were so young, barely scraping by. What were we thinking?" Addressing his silence and speaking softly, I added, "We can afford adoption now. Couldn't we make it the right time now?"

As Will looked at me, his expressionless face and empty eyes revealed no clue as to what he was thinking. Wondering if he had heard all my words, I added, "I really want to look into it."

"If we could get a lawsuit settlement, then we could afford it," Will finally responded, referring to a wrongful death lawsuit he was attempting to file against the Boy Scouts of America, the owner of the cabin where the Scouts had stayed, and the leaders charged with keeping Shawn and his fellow Boy Scouts safe. He added, "The attorney thinks we have a strong case."

I had argued against the lawsuit from the start. Although some would think Will had chosen a culturally acceptable place for his anger, I felt he had deceived himself into believing a lawsuit would soothe his pain. My thinking: *Who wins? We've already lost Shawn.* I didn't need to pin the blame on someone. Wouldn't it just resurrect my feeling that his accident could have been prevented? Maybe *I* could have prevented it. If I had told Shawn he couldn't join the scouts, then there would have been no camping trip for Shawn. Had I been an accomplice by supporting Shawn's desires?

"I don't want Pete or Ryan or Jay or any of Shawn's other friends to go through the agony of depositions and a trial," I had said to Will.

Neither Ryan nor Pete was with Shawn when his accident occurred, yet I knew it was probable they would be questioned if a lawsuit were to be filed. I felt the protective urges of a lioness whose cubs were in danger. I did not want any more trauma in my sons' lives. Ryan was too young to understand the process, but Pete was not. Weekly therapy seemed to finally be helping with Pete's anxiety, and I didn't want to do anything to jeopardize the progress he was making.

I was also concerned about Shawn's friend Jay. He had been with Shawn when he died. He witnessed the death of his best friend who was sitting beside him one minute, and then gone forever over the cliff's edge.

Only Jay knew what events had taken place in the seconds before Shawn fell and in the following horrific hours after. A few weeks after the funeral, Jay's mother, Pat, and I talked about that night. She told me how quiet Jay had been after the scout leaders brought him home from the camping trip. His dirty and tear-stained face was a sharp contrast to the bright and smiling one he had worn when she'd watched him walk out their door the evening before. She made a bath for him. And that is where he stayed, in the bathtub, for more than an hour.

"Please come out here and eat something. You must be hungry by now," Pat told him. As she spoke, Jay came around the corner and stared at the table. She filled his plate with hot food and urged, "Now, sit down."

Jay nodded, then slowly moved to the kitchen sink and started to wash his hands. The soap rolled over and over in his hands, small bubbles on his fingers and up his arms. Scrubbing, over and over…rinse. More scrubbing, over and over…rinse.

"Jay, what are you doing?" his mom had asked as she watched her son staring down at his hands. "You are clean. You just spent over an hour in the tub, Honey."

Jay turned, tears rolling down his cheeks, and spoke softly.

"Ma, I can't get the blood off my hands."

Pat's words had sent shivers down my spine and deepened the dark sadness that lay so heavily in my chest. Jay, like me, had guilt. Had he wondered if he could have pulled Shawn back? Or did Jay regret the play he and Shawn were engaged in when Shawn fell? I didn't want to make him relive those moments.

∞

I pulled my attention back to Will and our new world without Shawn. I could see Shawn's memorial tree, visible over Will's shoulder. It was sprouting new green leaves that blew gently in the spring breeze. Now, when Will mentioned the lawsuit, in spite of my thoughts and my desire to protect Ryan and Pete and Jay, I stayed quiet. *This time,* I said nothing. I waited for Will to continue.

"But I can't pursue the lawsuit without you." The tone in his voice unsettled me. It had the whiny sound of a young boy's begging plea, wanting to get his own way. Yet, when he added, "I need your signature. You're the mom," something inside me opened up. I *was* the mom, and the lawsuit couldn't be filed without my agreement. I knew my signature was the bargaining chip.

I looked directly into Will's eyes. "So, if I sign, you'll consider adoption." A statement made, not a question asked.

"If you sign, the decision of adoption is yours," Will confirmed. "After all, you'll be the mom."

Had we become like two children playing a game? *I'll trade you two of my green marbles for one of your blue marbles. The blue one I have long been looking for.*

I knew then I wanted to hold on to what we had left, so as not to lose any more. But I also wanted to rebuild and re-create. Over time, I grew to understand that Will and I were two grieving parents inexperienced with how to navigate through an immense loss; trying to forgive, to keep the peace, to compromise, and to smooth the edges of the jagged hole that was threatening to tear us apart. We were two parents, grieving differently.

But on that spring evening, with Shawn's scarlet maple tree visible over Will's shoulder, I focused on that blue marble.

And just like that, I traded my marbles for his.

Soon after this conversation, Will and I met with a social worker, Janice. Her office was three floors up in a large Victorian style home-turned-agency located a few blocks east of downtown Columbus. Sitting in her office, Will and I on ladder-back wooden chairs facing Janice as she sat relaxed at her desk, I started to feel a cautious excitement. Like a child seeing a big box wrapped in shiny paper. *Is it for me? Is there really some-thing good inside there for me?*

The completion of a home study took several months. We both had physical exams to take, detailed financial reports to complete, and individual autobiographies to write. Will partici-pated, but more in the manner of a reluctant student, completing the requirements necessary to pass a dreaded course. I was the star pupil, focusing on every detail of the process. I avoided seeking meaning in Will's behavior, for I was unwilling to enter-tain anything that might keep me from my dream of adopting a child.

The air was crisp and almost all the leaves had fallen from the trees the day the awaited package arrived from Children's Home Society and Family Services of Minnesota (CHSFS). From the envelope, I pulled the papers containing the information about the child with whom we had been matched and placed them on the kitchen table. On top of the packet sat two photos. Big dark eyes, staring back from a small, round, somber face, drew me in. Both photos appeared to have been taken when the baby was around seven months old.

In one photo, she was sitting bare-footed in a wooden high chair that was covered with Asian-appearing designs. She had skinny legs and black hair that stood straight up, adding a sense of fright to her face.

She was beautiful.

In the second photo, she was sitting on the lap of a fifty-ish-looking Korean woman who wore a matching somber expression. Maybe the foster mother? She held the little girl close to her chest, her hands forming a circle around the child's body. I held the photos in my hands and started to read the information on the first accompanying sheet. As part of the identification, under "Meaning of Name," it stated: "SeonKyung: to be good-natured and bright." Yet the little girl in the photos looked frightened and sad.

I was glad I was home alone when the package came. It felt exquisitely intimate to linger over the photos and read each word carefully. Korean words, which I was unable to read, were found next to many of the English words. In spite of the baby being referred to as "it," "female" was written in the spot designated to mark the child's sex.

"This baby was found crying in front of the children's home by a staff around 3 am on May 16, '84, when it wore pink cotton-clothes, wrapped in a pink quilt, with a slip of note in it, saying its birthdate." The intake history further explained, *"The head of the children's home supposed it more desirable for it to grow up in a normal home, rather than just in an institution."*

The papers stated that SeonKyung Jung had spent from May 17 to July 23 at the Angel Babies' Home of the Eastern Child Welfare Society due to a "congenital heart disease and cold." Biological mother and father: "unknown." Included were a medical summary, growth and development measures, and the result of an electrocardiogram. The Korean social worker's comments described her as "very cute, pretty, somewhat breathless," the word breathless suggesting to me she must be showing symptoms of her congenital heart disease. "We hope she will be matched with a wonderful family who could accept her with affection. Since intake, there has been nobody to come to see or inquire of her."

Since intake, there has been nobody to come to see or inquire of her. How could that be?

Even then, in my growing desire to have this child as my own, I understood she had another mother. A mother on the other side of the world who had lost a child just as I'd lost a child. But in this case, that other mother's loss would become my joy.

CHAPTER SIX

Heart Sounds

She marveled at how a heart with a hole that big kept beating.

~ Unknown

Arriving home late in the evening after picking up Laura at the Chicago airport, we were tired yet full of emotional energy. Laura had not slept during the drive from Chicago to Ohio, so I was hopeful that bedtime would go smoothly. I knew nothing about her sleeping patterns or the environment in her foster home in Korea. I had arranged her room like a typical sleeping area for a fourteen-month-old American toddler: crib, bookshelf, toys, and rocking chair. After feeding her and repeatedly rocking her and singing to her, I attempted to place her in her crib. Laura would not let go of me, her fists locked tightly onto my clothes or my hair. Eventually I ended up lying next to her on the floor of Ryan's bedroom. She didn't cry. She kept her solemn gaze. A gaze we later referred to as her "airport" look, a look she would wear only when overwhelmed with fear.

We both drifted off to sleep. In the early-morning hours, I awoke with a feeling of pressure on my chest. Not pain, but pressure. Pulling my brain awake, I tried to sit up. I suddenly realized that the pressure on my chest was not a premature cardiac event. It was Laura. She had snuggled up to me and ended up sound asleep on my chest. I'm sure she had jet lag. The only world she knew was thirteen hours ahead of us, making our nights her days. She may have slept in a family bed in her foster home. We did not know. Sleep was the biggest initial adjustment for her in coming to America—and for me.

∞

Will and I knew Laura had a heart defect before we agreed to adopt her, before we drove to Chicago to meet her. Since we had two healthy children when we applied for adoption, the agency tagged us as eligible only for a "special needs" child, leaving the healthy or very young infants for childless couples. We had checked "will accept" next to *surgically correctable heart defect* among the list of fifty-six different disabilities sent to us by our adoption agency.

It had been a daunting task—marking either: *will accept, will not accept,* or *possibly could accept*—next to defects, illnesses, injuries, or inflicted traumas that had enabled the bestowing of the label "special" on the needs of a faceless child. Burns, blindness, cleft lip, mental illness in the family, missing limbs, developmental delay, HIV-infected, uncorrectable heart defect, correctable heart defect. And the list went on. I only remember I marked "mental illness in the family" as *will not accept,* having learned from the early years of my nursing career spent in mental health how much genetic loading can impact a child. I marked "correctable heart defect" and "cleft lip" as *will accept.* Things that could be changed or fixed or mended appealed to me. After mailing the list back to the agency, I started to regret I had marked "cleft lip" as *will accept,* thinking that a noticeable defect in a child who already would stand out in a Caucasian family would make her adjustment more difficult. I felt more shame than regret, though, that I would entertain such a shallow thought.

I had been relieved when Laura's adoption packet arrived from Korea. The word "correctable" ran through my mind as I read the medical records stating she had a diagnosed heart defect—a ventricular septal defect (VSD)—commonly referred to as "a hole in the heart." "This is fixable," I said to myself. She was small and underweight for her age. Even though my medical specialty was not in cardiology, I knew enough to understand that her small, underweight size and the description of her as "somewhat breathless" were congruent with her VSD diagnosis.

The adoption agency wanted Will and me to learn what treatment information would be available for her in our community before we made the final decision to have Laura come to the United States. Without further word from us, she would remain in her foster home in Seoul. I gave Laura's medical records to our pediatrician, Dr. Lloyd Edwards. He told me he would review the records and consult with Dr. Douglas, a top pediatric cardiologist in Central Ohio.

Dr. Edwards and I had known each other for almost two decades by the time I turned Laura's Korean medical records over to him. We had met when I was a nursing student assigned to do an observation in his office. At the time, he was a tall, lanky, good-looking thirty-five-year-old with a quick sense of humor. I liked his soft-spoken manner and the way he talked directly to both the mother and the child. During my first pregnancy, I had pulled his information out of my student nursing notebooks and had chosen him as our pediatrician. Later, I worked with him as his office nurse and as a staff nurse in the nursery of a local hospital. He was my children's pediatrician, he was my colleague, and he was my friend.

"You realize, don't you," Dr. Edwards began when he

phoned me, "this child is very small for her age. Dr. Douglas believes her heart defect is severe enough to have affected her growth." I acknowledged she was small for her age but pointed out we didn't know her birth weight. He paused, then added, "Dr. Douglas believes you would be taking a big risk. He thinks there's a very bleak future for this little girl and recommends you do not adopt her."

He listened to my long silence before he softly continued, "Kathy, I think you and your family would be in for a lot of heartache and expense if you adopt this child. I'm sorry."

I thanked him for taking the time to consult with his colleague and for his kindness. He did not need to explain his words, for I knew this baby I wanted would probably need heart surgery and heart surgery is expensive. He was also telling me there was a great risk she would not survive. I heard his unspoken question.

Why would you want to risk loving and then losing another *child?*

After ending our conversation, I looked again at the pictures we had received in the packet from Korea. I stared at SeonKyung's dark eyes, her face already blended into the collage of our family photos. I viewed them each time I approached our refrigerator. How could I turn her away when she'd already been stuck with magnets onto my refrigerator door? *Don't worry, little girl, I'm not ready to give up on you just yet.*

There are perks to every profession. As a nurse, I cashed mine in to make an appointment with another cardiologist, Dr. Chan. I chose him because he was highly respected in our community. And because he was Chinese. He was ethnically as close to being Korean as I could find. In my eyes, that gave him high credibility when it came to evaluating the heart of an Asian child.

Will was working the day of the appointment with Dr. Chan and expressed no interest in going with me. So I met with Dr. Chan alone.

"This baby's weight is normal for a child of Asian descent," Dr. Chan told me. He added that repairing a VSD is "routine and not complicated here in the United States."

I interpreted his smile, the upbeat tone in his voice, and his this-is-no-big-deal attitude as a fist pump in the air telling me, "You go for it, Mama!"

I knew Lloyd Edwards was being protective of me. He had grieved with us. I understood why he preferred we "pass" on Laura and wait for a child who was not seriously ill. Dr. Chan did not know me or my son, Shawn. He had not seen my grief. He saw only my hope.

I reported Dr. Chan's more objective view to Will. He responded with his now familiar, "It's up to you. You're the mother."

Will left all the adoption decisions to me, leading me to feel both grateful at being in charge and burdened at being a party of one to Laura's adoption process. Although it shielded me from the awareness that Will was strategically disengaging from our family, it gave me the freedom to say yes to accepting SeonKyung Jung as our child. My daughter.

Our first spring with Laura, she and I spent the days alone together, with Will at work and Pete and Ryan at school. After a few weeks, I felt as though she had always been part of my life. When I carried her, she folded into my arms with the warmth and softness of a down comforter on a cold wintry day. She smiled to my smiles and quieted to the sound of my voice on those rare occasions when she would fret or whimper. The few Korean words she spoke when she had first arrived were quickly replaced with English. Her first full English sentence was "I love you," as she would place her tiny cool hands on my face and plant a wet kiss on my cheek.

Laura had arrived at the end of February, and the weeks passed quickly. Suddenly March 19, the second anniversary of Shawn's death, was upon me like a storm surge after a hurricane, having been brewing beneath in the cold deep waters of my grief. From the day Shawn had died, I talked openly about his death, wanting to give permission to others to share their memories with us and talk about how they missed him. Over the years, this has helped me stay afloat on the wave of grief that always starts a few days before, builds on the nineteenth, and carries me to the morning of March 20, when I can release my breath and move forward again. I've read that the date of the death of your child is "akin to a personal 9/11/2001." I have found that to be true. It's there every year and although each year is different, I figure out a way to make it through.

The year Laura arrived, though the March 19 grief hit me hard, the ache was milder and the plunge into despair was briefer and shallower. It was an unusual week. I was still at home on my three-month leave from work. Two days after the anniversary of Shawn's death, I turned forty. My co-workers, known for their love of practical jokes and humor, sent me a singing telegram. A very attractive young man rang my doorbell and burst into my home with an expanding bouquet of colorful balloons, singing lustily about my youth and beauty. Holding Laura, I stood laughing and feeling embarrassed. Her dark eyes grew bigger, taking in the bright colors and happy music.

I accepted Laura's giggle as permission to celebrate my birthday for a few minutes without feeling the guilt of having outlived my son.

A complete cardiology evaluation was a high priority for Laura after arriving in the United States. Was surgery needed? If so, when? Would she need other treatment? If so, what?

The first time I witnessed a professional listening to Laura's heart was when Will and I made the trip to Columbus Children's Hospital two weeks after Laura's arrival in our home. She was fifteen months old when she sat on a soft exam table in the office of Dr. Robert Douglas, the same doctor who had suggested we not adopt Laura. I had dressed her in a pale lavender jumper and had placed a matching bow in her hair, the purple ribbons contrasting with her shiny black hair. I was used to little boys. Dressing Laura was like dressing a doll. After pulling her clothes over her head and slipping her arms into a hospital gown to prepare for the exam, I held her close, feeling the beating of her heart.

The first person to enter the exam room was a young resident. As he started to examine her, Laura's eyes overflowed with tears. She held her breath, a response to fear that all parents dread. The sorrowful and loud sobbing that followed made it difficult for the resident to hear her heart and left me feeling helpless.

The resident gave an audible sigh of relief and stepped aside when Dr. Douglas entered the room. Standing a short distance away from the exam table, Dr. Douglas began to speak to a sobbing Laura. He spoke softly. Gentle words. His voice low, sounding almost as if he were humming. When her crying slowed to a soft whimper, he moved closer and placed the end of his stethoscope in her hands, the bright silver color catching her eye. Her small hands reached for it, moving her fingers along its smooth edge. Laura quieted and looked up into his eyes. Placing his hand over hers, he continued to talk, using English words she could not understand. But it was his gentle voice, the way he moved slowly toward her, that calmed her. With his hand over hers, as she held on tightly, he placed the stethoscope on her chest. With his skilled ears he listened; first at one spot, then another, and another, to the loud *swish-swish* of blood as it moved through the hole in her heart. His kind manner and Laura's response put me at ease, negating the fact he was the same man whose expert opinion had cautioned me against adopting Laura.

After Dr. Douglas's exam was complete, we spent the rest of the morning completing a list of tests: X-rays, blood draws, and heart studies. I carried Laura, clothed in her yellow animal-print hospital gown, as Will and I made our way through the walkway connecting his office building to the hospital.

The last stop before lunch was for her electrocardiogram (ECG) and echocardiogram (echo). The ECG would check for any electrical conduction problems in the heart by showing its electrical activity as line tracings on paper. The echo is a type of ultrasound test using high-pitched sound waves sent through a transducer that a technician would move around on Laura's chest. The echo is commonly used to diagnose a ventricular septal defect because it shows the size and shape of the heart and how the heart's chambers and valves are working. The pattern of blood flowing through the structures of the heart can be visualized.

The waiting room was crowded with children of all ages and their adult caretakers. Will and I sat close together on a bench while Laura shyly made her way toward other children to play. I had been so focused on Laura and her heart that my own heart skipped a beat when I saw a room full of other children and their illnesses, children tethered to oxygen, children unable to walk, and those too ill or weak to play. Near us sat a child with developmental delays who was having great difficulty talking. There were mothers alone with more than one child needing medical attention. I looked at Laura with her round little face full of color. Her legs, now filled out and no longer as skinny as they were in the first pictures we saw of her, were strong. They carried her where she wanted to go. And she was so smart. At fifteen months, she was already speaking Korean words and phrases. I knew her ECG from Korea diagnosed her VSD and she was symptomatic: small for her age, slow weight gain, sometimes breathless. Her hands and feet were always cold and she would sweat profusely from her head when she played. Yet, compared with the other children we were seeing at the hospital, I wanted to believe we had the healthiest child in the hospital.

I had been to Children's Hospital before, at least once with each of my three boys: Pete, to evaluate a mild concussion he acquired when he walked backward off a church stage, landing on the gym floor; Shawn, to repair the arm he broke after falling off the kitchen counter in an aborted attempt to reach the cookie jar; Ryan, to diagnose an ear infection that left him screaming and inconsolable in the middle of the night. All three events were common and fixable childhood predicaments.

As we waited and watched all the children playing, I began to wonder about Shawn. Wasn't there some part of Shawn that could have been saved? He would certainly have lost the vision in his right eye, for it had been smashed and obliterated when his face met the slate at the bottom of the ravine. Even if *he* couldn't be saved, what about using the cornea of his beautiful, blue, left eye to light the life of another child? It could have saved another child's sight, for it had remained perfect. Could he have survived if he had been reached sooner? What would life have been like for him—for us—if he had survived? Would his injuries have been fixable? But what about a brain injury?

Could I have prevented his fall if I had been there? I would have pulled him away from the edge. I felt a flood of anger that I never had the chance to protect him. Not a chance. Not even a chance to care for him or to fix his broken parts.

"Laura?" the nurse called out. I picked up Laura, and Will and I followed the nurse down the hall to cardiac testing. The room was cool and peaceful with friendly techs who made a game with the ECG stickers as they placed them on Laura's chest, arms, and legs. She lay quiet, focused on the brightly decorated ceiling above, while the machine recorded the size and movement of her heart. I knew her heart was broken, but I believed it was fixable.

The news Dr. Douglas delivered to Will and me when we returned to his office late in the day was what we expected, so it could not be labeled as good or bad. It just was.

"My opinion still is that she'll need surgery," he said. The day's testing confirmed Laura had a hole in her heart between the ventricles and her heart was enlarged. "We'll know more after a heart catheterization," Dr. Douglas informed us.

Although a heart cath is minimally invasive, requiring no large incisions, it's done under general anesthesia. During the procedure, a long, thin catheter would be inserted into a blood vessel in Laura's groin to be threaded through her body to reach her heart. A contrast dye would be injected in order to more clearly visualize the structure of the heart. Blood pressure and oxygen levels would be measured in the four heart chambers, pulmonary artery, and aorta.

Laura was scheduled to return for a heart cath in April. She would be sixteen months old. A tentative plan for the open-heart surgery was made for June.

Over the next month, I was busy with learning what Laura would eat, easing her into our sleep schedule, and introducing Laura to a growing number of friends and neighbors who wanted to meet her. When the day for the catheterization came, it was Pete, not Will, who accompanied Laura and me. Will did not want to take the time off work. Another step of Will's disengaging from the family? Maybe, but Pete had quickly become attached to Laura, and she to him, and Pete wanted to go with us.

Before Laura arrived in our home, Pete had expressed no strong feelings about adoption except to say, "She sure looks Asian," when he first saw her pictures.

"Yes, Pete, she does. That's because she *is* Asian," I had said with a smile.

Laura had arrived in our home on Thursday, February 27. On Friday, I started feeling ill with flu-like symptoms of nausea, fever, and body aches. Laura was very tentative and shy with

Will. His light hair, maybe? But she reached out for Pete and attached to him very quickly. At the end of the school day on Friday, Pete rushed home from school and, seeing that I felt very ill, took charge of Laura. Or maybe she took charge of him. He carried her everywhere he went. He played games with her, sang to her, and made her giggle. Late into the evening, when she would not sleep, he had her laughing and giggling in her high chair, eating rice pudding. As he headed out the door for school on Monday morning, he turned to me and, with his sixteen-year-old's wisdom, said, "You know, Mom, she really doesn't look very Asian to me at all."

By the time of the heart catheterization in April, Pete and Laura had the beginnings of a relationship that was more father-daughter than brother-sister. He was protective and he hated to see her cry. As soon as the corners of her mouth were drawn southward, predicting tears and a wail, he would pick her up and provide distractions to soothe her and stop her crying. "Mom, she can't cry like that! What if her heart bursts?"

Shortly after being admitted to the hospital, Laura was gurneyed from her bed in the cardiac unit to the catheterization suite. Pete and I headed to the cafeteria, me for a cup of tea and Pete for a muffin. We then toured the hospital. Pete walked with his hands stuffed deep into the pockets of his jeans, awkwardly shuffling his feet, making it obvious to passersby that he was a kid more at home on a soccer field than inside an academic medical facility. I tried not to focus on what I understood about the procedure, but I had problems pushing the picture of a catheter meandering its way through Laura's tiny body out of my mind. I worried it wouldn't fit, or would get stuck, or might even puncture her tiny vessels.

Pete made up silly songs, singing them quietly, tapping the rhythm on his knees. He'd strike up conversations with small children walking by, making goofy faces to make them laugh. All his efforts at blanketing his own anxiety eased my fretting mind during the seemingly endless wait for the procedure to be over.

Once Laura was taken to the recovery room, Dr. Douglas met with Pete and me. "The lung pressures are showing she is doing very well," he said, explaining that lung pressures are a crucial determining factor in doing the surgery. "She could wait. You wouldn't have to do this in June."

We had two choices. Laura could be scheduled to have the surgery in June, as had been previously discussed. "She would do better emotionally if done sooner, while she's still very young," he said. Or, we could wait until her size was a better match for the heart-lung machine that would support her during the operation. This would be when she weighed around forty pounds. For Laura, that probably would not be until she was almost five years old. "She would do much better physically if you wait until she is bigger, but that is often a tough age emotionally to undergo such extensive surgery."

I was surprised and thrilled. I thought about her small size. I wanted to give Laura the physical edge. I believed we had the ability to help her get through it emotionally when she was older. And the date when she would reach forty pounds seemed far into our future.

We decided to wait.

Family Time

We were a family of five again, but shaped differently after Laura joined our family. Our first outing as a refashioned family unit took place a few days after Laura arrived. We decided on eating out at Villa Nova, a popular, casual Italian restaurant in our community. It was usually filled with families, kids, and laughter and often was used by youth sports teams to celebrate a win or to prepare for a Saturday game with a carb-loading meal on a Friday evening. The hostess sat us at a table in the center of the larger of two main rooms. Although it felt strange to answer, "Yes, please," when asked if we needed a high chair, the crowded and noisy room gave me comfort as memories of past family events there flooded my mind. We decided that spaghetti would be a good choice for Laura, and we were served quickly by a staff that was adept at meeting the needs of large groups and spirited young kids. My concern that Laura might not find Italian food to her liking quickly vanished as I watched her focus on her bowl of spaghetti and then dive in with her hands. She was quickly covered with tomato sauce from ear to ear. Pete, Ryan, Will, and I were not the only ones laughing and giggling at her. I glanced around and saw many others in the restaurant smiling and laughing at our round-faced, dark-haired, tomato-smeared child. I imagined Shawn sitting next to Laura. His laugh would have been the most boisterous, his grin the widest.

With or without tomato sauce smeared on her face, Laura drew attention. When we were out for our daily walks at the mall during the cold month of March, we were often stopped by neighbors and passersby asking questions and commenting on Laura. She looked like a doll. Her petite body, smiling face framed by silky black hair, and her bubbly personality drew others to her.

Each family member formed a unique relationship with Laura. Whereas Pete had quickly become Laura's protector, Ryan was interested in sharing her with his friends. A few weeks after she arrived, he requested to take her to "show and tell" at school. After all, how many other ten-year-olds in 1985 had a baby sister from a foreign land? She offered more excitement than a new puppy.

Ryan already had caused a bit of commotion at school as a first-grader when he performed with a broom "guitar" singing "Centerfold" for "Share Your Music Talent Day."

Nah, nah nah nah nah naah…

Either his teacher did not know the song or did not think Ryan would know all the words and articulate them as well as he did. Since his broom/guitar did not make much noise, his voice was loud and clear.

My angel is the centerfold.

So this time I suggested that Ryan clear his sister as an object for "show and tell" ahead of time. It was a big hit. Ryan's fourth-grade classmates learned a little about the people and country of

South Korea, Laura loved the attention, and Ryan was pleased he was the expert on a subject about which his friends had little knowledge.

At the beginning of June, I returned to work, but Dr. Hamer was supportive of decreasing my schedule to three days a week, for which I was relieved. Jan, a friend and mother of two young children, became Laura's caretaker two days a week. Since Friday was an at-home day for Will, we decided that Friday would be my third working day on which Will would take care of Laura. I thought if he spent more time with Laura when I was not around, their relationship would deepen. I had noticed that when we were all together as family, I was the first person Laura would turn to for play or comfort. Will was always the last.

Janice, the social worker who had helped us with the first steps of our adoption journey, visited our home once a month to evaluate how Laura was adjusting. She left with the progress reports I was required to keep, recording Laura's physical growth, any new health problems, her language and social development, and documentation of any concerns we felt needed to be addressed. Her visits usually lasted an hour, and although they were always pleasant and uneventful, I had fears that something would go wrong. Something—I didn't know what—that would interfere with the finalization of our adoption. Adoptions are expected to be completed after the child has been in the home for six months, but because of some mix-up and delay with foreign adoption paperwork, it was nine months before Laura had her day in court. Although Janice kept reassuring me that, "Everything is good. It's just taking more time," I was ecstatic when a date to appear in court was set.

On November 19, 1985, Laura's adoption was finalized at the courthouse in downtown Columbus, Ohio. SeonKyung Jung acquired a new birth certificate with a new name that confirmed that Will and I were the parents of Laura Kathleen, born in South Korea on December 15, 1983.

Photos commemorate the event. In my favorite, Ryan, a gavel in his hand and a huge smile on his face, is seated at the large oak desk of the magistrate. I stand behind Ryan, holding Laura on my left hip. I'm dressed in beige and ivory, Laura in red. Both of us are smiling, looking peaceful and happy. Pete stands to my left, looking at the camera, face tilted toward Laura. Will, relaxed and smiling calmly, is beside me on my right. Janice, our social worker, is on his other side. Our group is flanked by an American flag on one side, an Ohio flag on the other, adding to the event's authenticity. It was more than a snapshot of one day. To me, it revealed a strong sense of accomplishment and determination that says, "The deal is done. This child is here to stay."

We celebrated Laura's second birthday ten days before Christmas. It would be our third Christmas without Shawn. The first Christmas had been empty, cold, and almost unbearable to endure. The second year had been hopeful with the anticipation of Laura's adoption. But in the third year, that first year with Laura, all the excitement of the holidays was ratcheted up a notch or two since we were celebrating them once again with a toddler.

During a shopping trip to the mall with Ryan and Laura for Christmas presents, I found myself chatting with a very friendly Santa Claus. Laura was hesitant and slightly fearful of Santa. But then he asked me about Laura.

I told him she had been adopted from Korea, and he then began to speak to her in Korean.

She pulled her head back and stared at him wide-eyed. But

she connected with his words and responded with a short Korean phrase. Hearing the familiar Korean sounds relaxed her slightly.

"I served several years in the U.S. military in South Korea," he explained to me.

Laura was then more willing to have her picture taken with Santa, but not without Ryan and me. That year's Christmas-with-Santa picture reveals how much my life had changed in two years: forty-year-old me, sitting on the knee of Korean-speaking Santa, my eleven-year-old son at my side, and my Korean-American, two-year-old daughter on my lap.

CHAPTER EIGHT

'Til Death Us Do Part

We are not the same persons this year as last year, nor are those we love. It is a happy chance if we, changing, continue to love a changed person.

~ W. Somerset Maugham, *The Summing Up*

Will hung at the edge of our family. Detached. He withdrew more and more from me, Pete, and Ryan and neglected to connect with Laura. His affection toward me declined and he became easily entangled in arguments with Pete. Will became so frustrated with Ryan's apathy toward playing sports that on a Saturday morning when Ryan announced he was done with playing on the sixth-grade football team, Will grabbed him by his shoulder pads and the belt of his pants and threw him into the van, announcing, "Yes, Ryan, you *will* play!"

I stood in the driveway yelling, "Stop it! Stop it, Will! Let him go!" My body tensed. My stomach lurched. I knew Ryan was struggling to be the athlete that Shawn had been and that Will wanted him to be, but his heart and body were just not up to it. I felt helpless and frightened as I watched Ryan's stunned face, his eyes brimming with tears, his voice silent. Will slammed the van door, jumped into the driver's seat, and drove away.

In social situations, Will would carry Laura in his arms and smile, appearing to be proud and happy with his daughter. But although he continued to watch her when I was at work on Fridays, he minimized contact with her when I was home. When she became ill with chickenpox that spring, she was feverish and fussy. She clung to me. I asked Will to go to the drug store and bring back some medicine so her fever could come down. Will's response was a curt, "No. Figure it out yourself," as he planted himself on our screened-in deck. His firm and deliberate sliding of the glass door completed the separation between us, shutting us out. Pete headed to the store while I turned my attention to fussy and feverish Laura.

Early in May, with the mounting negative family interactions, Will announced, "I just can't watch her anymore. You have to find someone else." He was lacking in any explanation but was adamant that he was done taking care of her, not only on Fridays but every day. "You need to be the one to dress her and take care of her. You or Pete can do that."

After Shawn's death, Will became an unhappy and angry man. I didn't know how to help him. I didn't know how to deal with his anger. Growing up as a middle child, I found I was happiest when I could talk things out or mediate a conflict. When that failed, I was quick to give in to the other person and ignore or not recognize my own anger. I managed my feelings by pounding them out on the piano, punching them out in an exercise class, or smothering them with a pint of ice cream. Barely twenty-one when we married, that was the approach I brought to our relationship. Will brought a passive-aggressive style. He did not raise his voice or engage in any verbal conflict. Instead, he would procrastinate completing a project or he would take an action that would force me into the position of needing to resolve a situation myself. We learned early in our marriage that our different styles of managing anger could be problematic. Once we had recognized this, we learned to talk things out and negotiate. This worked well enough for seventeen years, but after Shawn's death, we both reverted to the styles of our youth. Neither of us knew how to handle the emotions that accompanied our individual grieving.

Because of Laura's heart defect, her hands and feet would feel ice cold, so I set the heat a few degrees higher than we had in the past. One afternoon while Will was at work, I noticed our house kept getting colder and colder. When I called Will to tell him I thought we needed our furnace repaired, I learned that when he had discovered the thermostat was higher than what he wanted, he had extinguished the pilot light. "If you want the house this warm, then you can pay the heating bill," Will informed me, referring to my "fun" money that each of us kept that was separate from the family budget.

Will's old passive-aggressive style of dealing with anger had returned, but with a sharper edge of anger than I had ever experienced before. It made my stomach tighten. In turn, I responded with my old way of dealing with conflict. I signed up for extra aerobic dance classes, punching the air with my fists, pounding my feet on the gym floor. I took over paying the heating bill and Will agreed to reignite the pilot light. And I reverted by giving in to Will's refusal to care for Laura. I searched for other options for Friday childcare.

Who was this man Will had become? What happened to the Will who would spend hours with the boys engaged in a Monopoly game on a rainy Saturday afternoon while I went shopping with a friend? Or the man who had navigated our family bicycle rides through the park? *My* Will was a man who loved family traditions, gave thoughtful gifts on Christmas and birthdays, and helped the boys plan secret Mother's Day surprises for me. He had been a man who was known for his patience and thoughtfulness. A man who was happy with his world. I did not recognize this new Will; this irritable, angry, demanding person whom none of us in our refashioned family could satisfy.

At the end of May, Will joined his co-workers for what had become an annual whitewater rafting trip. I thought he might skip the trip because he seemed to be in such a deep funk. But he went, returning after three days sunburned, jubilant, and energized. As he had the previous year, he returned with two large group photos.

"Can you frame these for me like you did last year?"

Taking the photos from him, I saw small groups of men and women in rafts, only a few of whom I recognized. They were laughing and working together, the waters splashing all around them. The photos seemed designed to promote the "wet, wild, and wonderful" waters of West Virginia. In the center of one, Will's face beamed as he pulled on the oar he was holding, steering the raft downstream. I had not seen a look like that on his face for several years. A wave of resentment washed over me, followed by a small bit of shame. Why should I resent his being happy? It appeared the trip was good for him. Maybe it would help turn him around so we could reach each other again. *If he could be happy there, maybe he could be happy here again.*

"Sure, I'll get them framed for you. I'll have them match last year's frames and you can add them to your wall at the office."

❧

Three weeks after the whitewater rafting trip, Will stood in the doorway of our bedroom facing me and explained how he wanted a "sabbatical" from our marriage.

After he tried to get me to understand *why* a man who had been married since he was twenty, who had lost a son, and who had three living children would want to take a break for "a year or so" and "maybe go to California or something," he blurted out, "I care about you. I really do. I just don't love you anymore."

So that's how the conversation got started that June day. It had been more than three years since Shawn's accident. Even though the building blocks of destruction had been piling up during those years, I resisted any thought that a crumbling marriage could ever be a part of my world.

I believed I could not survive another loss.

I believed in forever.

I believed we could fix things.

I believed that not keeping our family intact would be equivalent to child abuse.

I heard Will's words very clearly, but the part of my brain that processes meaning pushed them away. I feared Will would do something impulsive—like leave us.

I wanted to believe he was reacting to all the stress of the last few years. We had endured so much as a family. So much change. Will did not do well with change. He liked consistency. He was comfortable with predictability. I also pondered the possibility that he might have a brain tumor. A brain tumor would explain the change in his personality. What else would make him think so irrationally?

Was it difficult for Will to utter those words? I'm not sure. "I just don't love you anymore." What does that really mean? What do you want to change? Do you love someone else? Are you tired of me? Not attracted to me now? Questions I dared not verbalize ran through my head. I didn't want to hear the answers.

Admittedly, I had been blind to so much. It was a protective blindness that had allowed me to function through the years after Shawn's death. Did others see it coming? I remembered my mother-in-law's warning two weeks after Shawn died. Watching me so focused and constantly worried about the boys during those first weeks after Shawn's death, my mother-in-law advised, "Pay attention to your husband. He needs attention or he will need to find it elsewhere." Had she seen this coming? I had no clue what she was trying to tell me. I remember feeling numb at the time. And I remember thinking, *I'm the parent. I'm supposed to be paying attention to my children.* And I wondered, *How can I pay attention to everyone all by myself?*

After Laura was adopted, I had felt a renewed trust in life, a renewed hope and happiness. But Will and I both built walls around ourselves. We functioned like toddlers in parallel play, side by side in two separate worlds. It was almost essential for our emotional survival after Shawn's death. Touching each other's grief was impossible as we tried to understand our own. When we tried to advance to cooperative play a few years later, we discovered we now had different goals. Different ways to fill up that hole to give our lives meaning...to live our lives so our son's life had meaning.

Me, I mothered. It comforted me and helped me focus on the future, calming the raging waves of the past few years. I tried to keep life as much like before as possible, or at least to appear like a normal family with a mom, a dad, three kids, a dog, and a cat. If our family appeared happy and vibrant on the outside, maybe it would permeate our insides and smooth some of the rough edges of the piercing hole left by Shawn's physical absence. But I assumed too much. I assumed Will's spending more time at work was his way of coping. And I interpreted wrongly: that his quiet and withdrawn moments were grief, needing time for himself; that his irritable, short verbal outbursts were temporary and harmless.

I responded to Will's announcement that he wanted a break from our marriage with, "Can we just go see a marriage counselor?" My question was a plea. If we saw a marriage counselor, I thought, it would buy some time. Time could help Will get his thinking straight. Time could teach me what more I needed to do to make Will happy and content. With time and a marriage counselor and us working together, we could fix this.

Will agreed to the counseling. "Let me go first," he said one day as he showed me the name of a psychologist he had found. His proposal that he talk with the therapist once or twice before we would all meet together seemed like an okay idea. At least it would get Will involved in therapy, which I initially thought he would resist. I felt hopeful.

Will went to two sessions alone and invited me to come to the third. We sat in stuffed chairs, forming a small triangle. The therapist started the conversation with something like, "Will and I have talked, and as I believe he has discussed with you, he is wanting to take a break from the marriage."

I began to realize I was not in a marriage counseling session. There had never been any intention to work at keeping our twenty-year marriage intact. I was the odd man out at a "your husband is telling you he wants out of this marriage" session. I was not sitting as part of a cozy trio, but I was on one side, alone. Totally alone.

"What can I do? How can I manage to take care of our family alone?" I asked, for I didn't know what else to say. I don't remember if I cried, but I remember feeling like I might throw up. My life was out of control.

The therapist's response was short. "The best thing you can do for yourself is to get a good attorney."

So I did.

An attorney friend of ours referred me to a colleague who was a divorce attorney. Chris was experienced in the anatomy of a failing marriage. I was not.

"How long has your husband been having an affair?" Chris asked at our first meeting.

Abruptly and with a bit of an attitude, I responded, "He's *not* having an affair." The question angered me.

"How do you know he is not having an affair?"

The question made me feel dirty, immoral, part of a world in which I didn't belong. "I know he's not having an affair because I asked him. And he said no."

Chris must have seen the fire in my eyes, for he looked down at the papers on his desk and moved on to other questions. By the time we met again four weeks later, I had completed my part of the paperwork for a legal separation. Handing the forms to Chris, I asked,

"How did you know Will was having an affair?"

I had learned a lot during that month. Most of it was painful.

"I just don't love you anymore," Will had said. Once those words were spoken and that announcement made, an avalanche of hurtful words, hidden betrayals, and new anxieties came sliding down, suffocating any chance of marital survival. My world became like the opening of the doors of a clearance sale: frantic, out of control, and then suddenly empty.

My knowledge of Will's affair came in the form of a phone call on a Sunday afternoon while Will was at work. "Your husband is having an affair with my wife," the distraught father of three little boys informed me. He had hired a private investigator. He had photos to prove that his twenty-six-year-old wife, a secretary in Will's office, indeed was involved with Will.

I also became aware that I had no fight left in me, at least not for this. I recalled a saying from a former nursing professor whose wisdom I valued. Her advice about the challenges of life: "Choose the mountain you're willing to die on." I was not in shape for yet another mountain.

In late August, Will packed up what he was taking to his apartment two miles up the road. As agreed upon, he took the TV, the gas grill, a computer, various pieces of furniture, and the photos of his whitewater rafting trip. Unframed.

Sadly, Bridgette, our much-loved family dog, went with him.

The good part—I always liked to find the good parts—was that Will preferred that I have full custody of the kids. His visitation with the children was stated simply in our legal document: "Visitation will be in the best interest of the child." And he agreed the kids and I would remain in the home we owned. His only child-support payment was the monthly mortgage. Will wanted as little responsibility as possible, as much "freedom from the past" as legally allowed. Almost a decade would pass before we found ourselves in court again, taking another look at visitation and child support.

Six months. From June to mid-December. The marriage was

over. Done. Gone. On December 17, two days after Laura's third birthday, dissolution papers were signed. Our marriage was officially terminated.

The divorce was difficult and painful. There were tears and drama and anger in the months surrounding the divorce. I was confused about life, worried about the kids, afraid I would run out of money, fearful of the future. Although I believed I had already gone through the most horrific experience of my life and I knew I would survive my divorce, I sometimes felt God was leaning way too hard on me. More than once during the early years of navigating life as a single parent, I raised my face to the heavens and shouted: "Why me? Why this? Why now?"

CHAPTER NINE

Light Up My Life

....

I said: What about my heart? He said: Tell me what you
hold inside it. I said: Pain and sorrow.
  He said: Stay with it. The wound is the place where
the Light enters you.

~ Rumi

....

Two weeks after the dissolution papers were signed, I rang in the new year as a single parent. Our refashioned family unit of five was cracked, shattered, broken. It had gone out of style. I was a single parent of four children: Laura had just turned three, Ryan was plodding his way through the sixth grade, Pete was looking ahead to his high school graduation in June, and Shawn had been gone for three years and ten months.

If anyone asked me if I was married, I would reply that I was a single parent. I hated the word *divorced*. "Divorced: to be separated from things to which you were once connected or associated. To disunite. A separation. Especially one that is total or complete." I did not want that word to define me.

Years later, I read on Wikipedia the best description of the *me* I was back then. "Single parent: an uncoupled individual who shoulders most or all of the day-to-day responsibilities for raising a child or children." I was uncoupled. And there were many days when my shoulders and my heart could testify to the weight of it all.

If I were to map out the events of the first years after my uncoupling, I would place myself on an unpaved road, a

68

winding road with sharp curves punctuated by potholes, flying rocks, and strong winds pushing me to the edge. There was the constant balancing of financial struggles and the navigating of Pete and Ryan through the emotional terrain of a now-fatherless household.

Pete was preparing for life after his graduation, which involved me driving him to visit colleges in Indiana and Ohio. But at least he seemed to be benefiting from continued counseling and was doing well.

Ryan was struggling. In the weeks after Will moved out, Ryan's entire being slowed down. He finished his schoolwork at a snail's pace, he walked in slow motion up the street to school, and his favorite activity was sleeping. Some mornings, as Ryan sat motionless on a kitchen chair, I would tie his shoes for him to help him get out the door to school. My eleven-year-old's depression was screaming for help. Help came to him in the form of individual sessions with a child psychologist, followed by an hour of group work focused on schoolwork and peer support.

At Ryan's intake session, the psychologist asked Ryan to draw a picture of his home. As the psychologist handed the picture to me at the end of the evaluation, the massive weight of Ryan's depression pressed deep into my chest, pushing out a guttural, *Oh, my God*. Ryan's "home" showed a small house with a door, no windows, sitting in the middle of the paper. The house had no ground to sit on, it floated in mid-air. Figures representative of me, Ryan, Pete, and Laura stand to the side of the house. I am the largest. I stand with my arms at my side, away from my body, and hands splayed open. I have tears on my face and my hair streaks out from my head, looking as if I have just put my finger in a powerful electrical socket.

In the tell-me-about-your-picture phase of the evaluation, Ryan's response was, "I'm worried about my mom. If something happens to her, then I will have nobody to take care of me." I could barely breathe.

Ryan desperately needed the individual and group therapy sessions. And I needed the twenty-five-minute crosstown, rush-hour, twice-weekly drive. It made me feel like I was doing "something" to fix him. It became a cathartic lifeline to which I clung in order to revive Ryan's joyful soul.

The summer before Pete went to college, there was one glimmer of good news. The lawsuit against the Boy Scouts of America, that black cloud looming above me, lifted, culminating in an out-of-court settlement the day before the trial by jury scheduled for July 1, 1987—the day we should have been celebrating Shawn's sixteenth birthday. Equal amounts of money were to be disbursed to Will and to me, and the bulk of the settlement was to be placed in a trust fund for Pete and Ryan's college educations.

A few weeks later, when we met to sign the final settlement papers, Chris, my divorce attorney, was with me. He was giving me *pro bono* lessons on how to stand up for myself and my children. Since Laura had not yet been born when Shawn died, Will felt she had no legal right as a beneficiary of the lawsuit. But Chris found a detail in the Ohio Revised Code pertaining to wrongful death lawsuits that stated that any child *conceived* prior to the death of the person on whom the lawsuit was based has a right to funds. Shawn died March 19, 1983, and even though Laura was not adopted into our family until February 27, 1985, she was born on December 15, 1983. Laura could have been *conceived* four days prior to Shawn's death. Three months later, when the money was disbursed, money went into a trust fund for Pete and Ryan, and a small amount went into a savings account designated for Laura and to be managed by me. The small amount of money was enough to pay for some future textbooks for a year or so in college; its value was not in the amount, but in the message meant for Will.

∾

Even though I was rarely alone as a single parent, I was often lonely. And I was also worried about my own health. I had developed a growth on my thyroid gland. In the spring following my divorce, I had a radioiodine scan and started medication to treat the nodule, but that rocketed me into an overactive state, forcing me to deal with heart palpitations, shortness of breath, intestinal distress, and an overall feeling of apprehension and dread. On the plus side, I had more energy, albeit nervous energy, and I ate constantly while continuing to lose weight.

In late September, I visited my endocrinologist again. "Since four months of medication isn't helping," he said, "the next step is to get a biopsy." The look he saw in my eyes was not surprise but fear, for I could see and feel the lump in my neck getting bigger. My doctor quickly added, "I'm not suspecting anything serious, but just to be safe. The biopsy is quick and easy, and the needle's very thin. You'll barely feel it," he added, hoping to alleviate my anxiety.

He was correct—the needle was thin—but he hadn't told me it was about five inches long. Even so, the surgeon was quick and skilled, resulting in a procedure that was less uncomfortable than when I had my ears pierced in college using a syringe needle and ice cubes.

I was at work when the surgeon's office called me about the biopsy results. "Kathleen, the doctor would like to discuss the results of your biopsy. Can you come to our office tomorrow?"

"Can you please give me the results over the phone?" I asked, knowing she'd deny me that option. When she responded that she could not do that, I wanted her to know I knew their little tricks. "Well, obviously, that means the biopsy is not normal, or you would not ask me to come in. So, could you just tell me?" My overly assertive words surprised me, but they did nothing to help me avoid a trip to the surgeon the next day.

"Atypical cells" was the result of the biopsy. Meaning, there were not enough abnormal cells to diagnose cancer, but because the cells obtained from the needle aspiration were abnormal, they were not considered benign. I was scheduled for surgical removal of my thyroid, a total thyroidectomy. I'm not sure which was my greater fear: not surviving the surgery or the possibility of finding out after the surgery that I had cancer.

When I was nine, I had the mini-trauma of seeing my mother in the hospital after she had thyroid surgery. My aunt had snuck us in to see her. Stupid idea. I remember being taken in through a back door of the hospital and entering my mother's room near the exit. I stood and looked at her, needles in her arms, eyes half closed, and a large packing with ice placed across her neck. I don't think I had even seen my mother asleep before that. She was always up, dressed, makeup and happy smile on, and enjoying her second pot of coffee by the time I first saw her in the mornings. It was a miracle to me when she came home the next week, looking like the same mom as before she went into the hospital—before she lay dying. The nine-year-old me pledged, "I will never let someone cut *my* throat. Never."

I broke that pledge to myself, reviewed my updated will, and invited my mother to spend a week with her grandchildren in our home at the end of November. Once again, she was there for me with her quiet strength. I often describe my mother as quiet, but that is not to be confused with passive. She could be a real tiger, especially when it came to her children and grand-kids. She was sitting in my hospital room beside my bed when, a few hours post-op, in walked Will. He had papers related to the lawsuit, financial papers that would release money. My signature was an urgent need for Will.

If my mother could have transformed herself into a lion, she would have pounced on him. She got up from her chair and stood by my bedside, placing her cool hand on my arm, puffing up her small five-foot-two frame to the max. I imagined I saw fire sparking out from her blue eyes and the hair on the back of her neck rising up.

"What are you doing here?" Her words to Will were icy. The muscles in her face tightened; her mouth twitched. Will stam-mered and stuttered, bit his lip, and shuffled his feet, reminiscent of seventeen-year-old Will when his dad came to rescue us from a secluded spot in the park after Will's car battery had died while we were kissing on a cold wintry night. But we were no longer seventeen, but forty-two. It was not Will and I together facing his father, but Will and I apart, my lion-mother at my side.

I signed the papers, then said to my mom after Will left, "It's okay. Anything I sign today probably could be contested since I'm under the influence of anesthesia and pain meds." I was just relieved to be on the other side of the lawsuit and the other side of my surgery. Alive.

The final diagnosis was chronic thyroiditis. All tests post-sur-gery were benign.

My mother and I shared matching scars: pale-colored, thin smiles resting just above our collar bones, beneath our fiery blue eyes.

Laura was a bright light shining in my life. She was, as her Korean name proclaimed, "bright and good-natured." At three, she was happy, warmly affectionate, and always questioning. She loved being near me, skin touching skin. She loved words and books and talking. An early talker, she often surprised me with her vocabulary and inquisitiveness. Not only were our conversations intense and filled with endless questions, but she also would engage others in endless conversation, dialogue, or interrogation. She interviewed the older couple sitting behind us at a Cincinnati Reds baseball game and the woman next in line at the grocery store. When I took Laura to the barber who trimmed her bangs, she would eagerly jump up in his barber chair, grinning at her own reflection in the mirror. He'd ask, "Well, what's going on with you today, Sweet Pea?" And Laura would open up a running monologue about our family life. Others in the shop chuckled as I encouraged him to cut faster.

As I was learning my new role as a single mom, Laura was questioning and defining her own identity. Her heartbeat was part of her identity. The sound of her beating heart reminded Laura of the *crunch-crunch* her boots made in the snow. She had her own stethoscope, which she liked to wear draped around her neck. It was not a toy, but a bright red, authentic stethoscope that had hung around my neck in the early days of my nursing career. She'd place it on the chests of her doll, her brothers, herself, and me, comparing sounds.

We would travel down to Children's Hospital, just Laura and I, every six months, then yearly, repeating the tests that had been performed the first day in Dr. Douglas's office. We added it to the list of routine check-ups, like dental cleanings and school physicals, making it a mother-daughter day, with lunch and a trip to Borders bookstore or a downtown shop.

Just as Laura learned her heart sounded different from other people's hearts, she also became aware her eyes were shaped differently from those of myself and her brothers. Laura was three years old when she perched herself on the edge of the bathroom sink, her elbow parked near my collarbone. "Mommy, why don't my eyes open up all the way like yours do?" She moved closer to my face in an effort to get a more intimate look.

"They do open up all the way. Your eyes and my eyes have different shapes," I told her.

Laura turned her face away from mine. She opened and closed her eyes, studying them intently in the mirror above the sink. She turned her face back to me and watched as I finished putting mascara on my eyelashes. Planting both her hands with their soft coolness on my cheeks, she pulled my face toward hers, stopping when our noses touched.

"Why, Mommy? Why's that? 'Cause I'm 'dopted?"

A few months later, she decided to be a fairy princess for Halloween. Laura was all decked out in pink ballet slippers, a matching gown with an attached tutu, a sequin-studded headband, and a sparkling magic wand. This became her main attire for days before and after Halloween. Slipping on her tights and clutching her magic wand released a momentum that kept her in constant motion—leaping, twirling, and dancing all through the house. The wand was always attached to her right hand, ready to perform its magic at the flick of her wrist. Of course she wore it to preschool. Daily. Reaching into her cubby one afternoon, I felt the tip of her wand poking my shoulder. Poke-poke, followed by another poke-poke. The third poke-poke came with an exasperated, "It's not wooking! Mommy, it's just not wooking!"

Turning and looking at her over my shoulder, I asked, "What do you mean, 'It's not working'? What do you want it to do?"

With a stomp of her little pink foot and a shake of her now slightly worn tutu, she replied, "I'm trying to turn you into Kor-ee-an, Mommy, and it's just not wooking!"

"Oh, so that's the problem," I said, glancing at her wand with its bent edges and missing sparkles. Could it be losing some of its magic? "Sorry, Honey, I'd like that too. I just don't think it's going to work today." I didn't want to dash all her hopes.

At preschool, Laura had become close friends with Jonathan, a little boy of Taiwanese descent. His mother usually brought him to school, and one day Laura pointed her out to me, dragging me by the hand across the school parking lot. "There's Jonathan's mommy. See?" Jonathan's mommy was a beautiful, dark-haired Taiwanese woman who responded sweetly to Laura's stares and the tugging on her coat sleeves.

In the car one day, Laura informed me, "I wish you looked like Jonathan's mommy." I smiled. Good thing I wasn't too sensitive about my looks. I was pleased she wanted to change me and not herself.

I knew inevitable questions would arise about how she looked compared with how I looked. But so soon? She was barely three. Laura began to ask questions that required more than just a smile or an "I'd like that too" to satisfy her. By kindergarten,

to have a family with a mother and a father and her brothers all under one roof. A family. Instead, her father lived somewhere else while her two brothers and her mother were all in therapy.

∾

In the beginning months of my therapy with Dick and during the first year after our divorce, our children's visitations were sporadic and only for brief periods during the day. Pete turned eighteen and graduated high school five months after our divorce and had little interest in spending time with his father. But Will would take Ryan and Laura to McDonald's or on an outing such as picking out pumpkins at Halloween.

A year after our divorce and a few months after Laura's fourth birthday, Will married Irene, a woman he had started dating after moving on from his twenty-six-year-old coworker. Will and Irene lived a twenty-five-minute drive from us with Irene's two boys. Since their home offered more space than Will's small one-bedroom apartment, overnight visits were introduced into the visitation schedule at Will's suggestion. Once a month or so, Ryan and Laura would each pack a bag with clothing and a toothbrush. I would drive them to Will's and he would bring them home the following day. I dreaded the drive, a 6 p.m. Friday evening crosstown annoyance in the rush-hour freeway traffic.

Initially Laura, with my help, would get ready for the visit willingly, eagerly, and with her typical joyful enthusiasm for adventures. Ryan was resistant. He'd try to bargain with his dad, usually unsuccessfully, to go out with his friends in lieu of an overnight at Will's. This behavior, I felt, was typical of being a just-turned-thirteen-year-old boy. After three or four months of overnight visiting, Laura's willingness to visit her dad changed. She would procrastinate getting her things together and move with the speed of a slug out the door and into the car. No matter what I said, I was unable to obtain an explanation from Laura or get her to talk about her feelings. Ryan's back-seat lack of enthusiasm and Laura's sad-faced silence sitting next to me made the drive to Will's seem twice as long.

I sat in Dick's office one cold wintry Monday sharing the events of Laura's and Ryan's previous Friday night visit. When they arrived home Saturday evening, Ryan had shuffled off to his room. Laura and I had headed to the bathroom to begin her bedtime ritual.

"I don't want to go back to Daddy's house anymore," Laura tearfully told me as the water filled the tub. Laura had asked after the two previous visits if she would have to go back again. But this was the first time she expressed not wanting to return. And this was the first time she cried when talking about it.

"Why's that?" I asked.

"A monster lives at Daddy's house," Laura explained as she swung her legs over the edge of the tub and then submerged herself under the water. Coming up for air and wiping the water from her face, she continued, "A monster with a mustache lives there."

Mechanically I helped her with her bath, watching her naked Barbie dolls bob around in the water. I thought about Will's home. I had been no further than the front entranceway. I knew Ryan and Laura slept in separate places in the house, each on a sofa or pull-out bed. But I had never been shown the sleeping places. I thought about who slept in Will's home. Will, Irene, Ryan, and Irene's sons, one a year younger than Ryan and one two years older. I had not met Irene's boys. Was Will the only person in the home with a mustache?

When Laura had climbed out of the tub, I helped her as she patted herself dry, wrapped herself in a towel, and headed across the hall to her room. She pulled her nightie over her head and searched her shelf for a book for us to read. "Can we read three tonight, Mommy?"

I nodded. "As many as you want," I told her as she crawled up on my lap in the rocking chair.

The warm water had calmed her as she moved her small body back and forth in our large tub. But as I had watched the water lapping back and forth, I thought of her tears, her fears, her monster, her request to not sleep at Will's home again. And I thought about my lack of knowledge of what Will's home was like for Laura.

"I don't want to sleep over at Daddy's again," she told me again mumbling, and this time without the tears. Then she added, "The monster scares me at night when I try to go to sleep."

A shiver went down my back. Bile rose up in the back of my throat.

Laura listened to the words of her favorite books. When all the stories were read, we continued to rock. With our arms entwined and her weight against my chest, I could feel Laura's muscles relax and her breathing change. She quickly fell into a deep sleep. As her breaths deepened, so did my understanding that Laura was learning that not all places in her world felt safe and carefree and filled with love.

"Will is not willing or able right now to be the father Laura needs," I told Dick as I ended the telling of the weekend events.

Dick's voice was soft. Calm. The silence in the room was warm.

When I left his office, another appointment card in my hand, I didn't want to leave and walk back into my world. In my world, it was my job *alone* to parent my children. I longed to stay in the corner of Dick's office and feel the sun warm my face. To listen to someone tell me, "It's going to be okay. It's going to be okay."

I fought against the guilt that penetrated me. I had failed to protect Laura. I could have looked closer at where she slept at Will's. I could have listened and remembered his words: "I just can't watch her anymore. You have to be the one to dress her and take care of her."

As Dick and I had discussed, I shared Laura's monster report with Will. I told him of her increasing fear about staying at his house. I felt relief when Will responded, "Let's not have Laura stay here overnight."

We both agreed on *no* overnights. Visits of a few daytime hours once or twice a month, at least for now, and only when Ryan was there too.

I found the best therapist I could for Laura. Laura told her story while playing with dolls, then hugged her therapist goodbye and skipped toward me at the end of each session.

"She's very angry at the daddy doll," the therapist told me before describing how Laura would place the daddy doll in the corner, face down, while she and the mommy and brother dolls would interact. Laura picked out the black or purple crayon when she colored. I wondered, *Are there other colors to choose from?*

Several months later, I took a trip to the beach with friends. Amazing pleasure washed over me as I stood atop a sand dune for the first time in my life. I cried. Then guilt revisited me in waves.

"This should be Shawn standing here. Not me," I whispered to my friend. "Shawn didn't live long enough to stand on a sand dune."

Deep sorrow and regret washed over me. I had failed to protect Shawn. I could have looked more closely at where he would be camping. I could have said, "No, Shawn, you cannot go on this Boy Scout trip."

❧

Laura didn't talk about the monster very often, but when she did, I listened. "Maybe he was in my dreams," she told me when she was a teenager. "I really don't remember." Over the years, I came to view her monster as symbolic of her struggle with figuring out the kind of relationship she wanted with Will.

❧

I returned often to my safe place in the quiet corner of Dick's office. As the sun filtered in through the window, I sank deeper into therapy.

Questions remained. What really happened that Saturday afternoon in March in Hocking Hills as Shawn tumbled down from the cliff? What really happened that night at Will's house? *What really happens when I am not there to protect my child?*

And as I rocked Laura each night before bed, I yearned for someone to pick me up and rock me.

PART TWO

Those who are close to us, when they die, divide our world. There is the world of the living, which we finally, in one way or another, succumb to, and then there is the domain of the dead that, like an imaginary friend (or foe) or a secret concubine, constantly beckons, reminding us of our loss.

~ Azar Nafisi, *Things I've Been Silent About: Memories*

The despair you now feel with a missing child is overwhelming.

Very different from the grief you experienced when Shawn died. You miss Shawn terribly, yet you believe you know where he is. With time, you have learned to live with the constant beckoning from Shawn's world. Some days the call is loud, most days just a whisper. A tap on your shoulder.

You don't know where Laura is. You miss her. You grieve for her.

Your body fails you. You have shooting pains from a bulging disc in your lower back. Walking is impossible. Painful. You position yourself on the floor of your bedroom, hoping the hard surface will ease the pain. Your stomach burns from too much ibuprofen. Lying next to the sliding glass door of your balcony, two stories up, phone near your ear, you close your eyes. Visions of you leaping off the balcony play against your eyelids. You open your eyes and see it more vividly, an intrusive animation. Your heart races, sending waves of paralyzing panic through your body.

For you, mothering is a balancing act between keeping your children safe and letting go. Do you need more courage than most mothers to do the work of mothering? To know when to hold on tight to your child and when to let them spread their wings and fly? Is this yet another price you pay because your child has died?

"Be strong," you tell yourself. "You must stay focused."

You need to find Laura.

CHAPTER ELEVEN

Coming Together

....

*Confluence. Things come together. The right ingredients
and suddenly: Abracadabra!*

~ Neil Gaiman, *Smoke and Mirrors:
Short Fictions and Illusions*

....

Balancing the budget on a thirty-hour-a-week office nurse position became increasingly more challenging for me. Cost for a month of daycare for Laura added up to more than a semester's tuition for Pete at The Ohio State University. The summer before Laura began kindergarten, my friend Syl started filling me in with bits and pieces of information about a new psychiatric inpatient unit for children at The Ohio State University. Syl, a nurse recruiter, knew I had begun my nursing career on an adult psych inpatient unit at OSU. As many nursing careers do, mine had transitioned to fit the needs of my family and lifestyle. My career had taken me from inpatient adult psych, to newborn nursery, to neonatal ICU, to mother-infant, to teaching Lamaze childbirth classes in the community, to pediatric office nursing, and to OB/GYN nursing in Dr. Hamer's private practice for the last ten years.

"With your experience, this job is perfect for you," Syl said with excitement.

The timing of my financial needs merged with the growing attention to the mental health needs of children in our community. Confluence. Things came together, and a few interviews later I started working full time on the child psychiatric unit at

OSU. It was an exciting opportunity to be part of the genesis of new research in children's mental health and new inpatient protocols. During the years I worked on the child unit, I labeled it "the best" job I had ever held. Even in reflection, my five years on the child psych unit at OSU stands out as a highlight of my career, one that later would influence me to advance my education to become a nurse practitioner.

My new job came with a more complex schedule to juggle. I was hired with the understanding that I would rotate two months of day shift with one month of night shift. During the months I worked days, I would be expected to clock in at work by 6:55 a.m. and I would leave after the shift report was completed at 3:30 p.m. or later. My night shifts had the expectation that I would arrive by 10:55 p.m. and leave after the report to the morning shift after 7:30 a.m. I started the job in July. Pete, at the age of twenty, was taking college classes and living at home. Ryan was fifteen and getting ready to enter his sophomore year in high school, and Laura would start an all-day kindergarten at her daycare center in September.

Pete, Ryan, Laura, and I all had our own independent and interdependent roles. We needed each other and relied on each other. Our days were long, starting with Ryan's before-school paper route to deliver The Columbus Dispatch and ending with homework and preparing for the next day. The in-between hours were filled with work for Pete and me; school for Pete, Ryan, and Laura; piano lessons for Laura; baseball practice for Ryan; and band practice for Pete. And, of course, all the expected and unexpected events that accompany family life. There were a few bumps in the road, such as Ryan falling back to sleep on more than one occasion after the papers were delivered and not making it to school on time. And the time I decided to take a "short nap" after work before stopping for Laura and being awakened two hours later by the daycare staff calling me. "Did you forget to pick up Laura?" they queried. But we soon fell into a predictable and mostly smooth routine. And amazingly, despite our many imperfections, things did come together.

∽

Laura continued to focus on her identity. As she started elementary school, she exhibited a growing curiosity about her birth mother. We had no photos of Laura before the age of fourteen months, except for the three photos from the adoption agency and her small passport photo. And we had no photos of Laura's birth mother.

When Laura was six, she drew her own portrait of a woman she had no memory of seeing. The picture, drawn from Laura's heart, shows a woman facing forward. She has a round face, short hair, and bangs across her forehead drawn with a thick, black crayon. The picture stops at her waist. She is wearing a blouse Laura colored in with heavy strokes of her red crayon. Birth Mother's eyes are round and black and are looking straight ahead. Noticeable are the big oval tears dotting both cheeks. Laura labeled her picture *My Birth Mother, When She Left Me.*

"Maybe if I go to Korea, I could find my birth mother," eight-year-old Laura announced one day as we were driving to or from someplace together. Until then Laura had been silent, sitting beside me as I drove. Before I could respond, she started to giggle.

"Mommy, that's almost impossible." I stopped at a red light and looked at her with a questioning gaze. "Everyone over there is going to look alike," she explained.

Then we are both started laughing. "Well, that's kinda true," I agreed.

"Mom?"

"Yes, Laura?"

"What if I'm a twin? There would be someone in Korea who looks just like me!"

I looked at her face, all lit up in a beaming smile. I smiled back, then turned my head and focused my eyes on the traffic light. It turned green. I shifted into first gear. For a moment, I engaged my mind in her fantasy of another little girl who looked just like Laura. I smiled.

"Fat chance, Honey. Fat chance," was my response.

$$\infty$$

Our trips to Children's Hospital for Laura's cardiac evaluations were stretched from every six months to a yearly event as Laura's reports consistently showed an increasingly stronger heart.

When Laura was close to nine years old, and right before Christmas, I stood next to her and listened to the silence as Dr. Douglas placed the earbuds of his silver stethoscope in his ears. His exam was the last step, ending the long day of tests and evaluations. He warmed the bell end with his hands, before placing it on Laura's chest. He paused briefly at each spot he placed his scope, head tilted, eyes intent, before moving and listening to another spot, then another, and another. He let the bell rest in his hands and took a step back from the exam table. He smiled.

"Well, Laura, it looks like you will never need heart surgery after all. You are a very healthy girl."

It was the best Christmas present ever.

Laura grinned while I listened intently as Dr. Douglas gave his medical explanation. As Laura was growing, the tissue of her tricuspid valve had partially covered the hole. This partial closure occurs in less than one-third of children over the age of six and very rarely after the age of ten. Having heart surgery could put her at more of a risk than living with an unrepaired VSD.

"You will always need to take care of yourself, Laura, but you'll do fine without surgery."

CHAPTER TWELVE

Love Me Tender, Love Me True

If, when two families merge, you take the metaphor of "blending" literally, you recognize that there are variable speeds on your blender and that you can easily set it not to blend but to grate, chop, or shred instead. It all depends on what you program it to do.

~ Robert Root, *Happenstance*

When I was first divorced, I felt the need to run to the window and breathe in fresh air when anyone mentioned dating. I had too much on my plate without navigating the terrain of a new relationship. I had learned to enjoy the freedom and independence that came with being single, even with the increased responsibility that was part of solo parenting. And I had built a protective emotional wall around myself, avoiding the inevitable task of learning to trust again.

Very slowly, and after more than four years of being single, I started to think about dating. After a year or so of random dating experiences that gave me a glimpse of a future I knew I didn't want, I took a risk and joined a dating service. My hope was that a dating professional could, by learning all about me, go out and search and hunt down my ideal man, like a trained German Shepherd tracking down a wandering child.

Great Expectations was a pre-internet way of meeting a partner. From reviewing pictures, a written profile, and a short video, I agreed to meet up with a guy named Kevin. I had learned that we both loved music and books and that he shared custody of his daughter, Elizabeth, who was eighteen months older than Laura. I laughed out loud when I read, "I'm seeking a woman who is responsible for her own happiness." That told me a great deal about his past relationship. And although I certainly fit that criteria, I wondered if it ever occurred to him that there might be others who were counting on *me* for *their* happiness? But he was a dad, so certainly he would understand.

I found Kevin waiting for me, sitting in the café end of Borders bookstore, reading *The New York Times*. I was more than twenty minutes late. My excuse of being slowed down by a train was legitimate. He later admitted he was getting ready to leave, thinking I had stood him up. We were both nervous. We were both tentative about trusting someone. My recent dating experiences had varying degrees of satisfaction, but each one helped me clarify what I wanted and needed in a partner. Kevin had been divorced a year, after a long and drawn-out separation, most of the conflicts centering around his ten-year-old daughter.

Our conversation was cautious that Sunday afternoon; both of us wanted not to seem too interested. I liked that he looked at me as we talked, his brown eyes soft and kind, his voice calm and quiet. He seemed to be listening. I liked that I found him reading *The New York Times* and that he had waited for me.

We parted with me saying I needed to pick up a book for Pete for Christmas. "I'm looking for Benjamin Hoff's *The Tao of Pooh*," I told him.

Kevin's response, "Oh, that's a great book. Your son should love it!" made it easier for me to make plans to meet the following Wednesday to go walking.

The few hours at Borders were the only heedful moments in our relationship, for it took off faster than a Korean bullet train.

We both felt an easy connection, and even though our careers were very different—me a psychiatric nurse and Kevin a database administrator for *The Columbus Dispatch* Printing Company—our personalities and what we valued in life matched. Standing beside his waterbed on the first night I spent in his apartment, waiting as he emptied his bed of book after book after book to make room for me, I knew I had found my soulmate.

Kevin and I met on November 22, became engaged at Christmastime, and married six months later, on May 22, 1993. My words of caution to Pete and Ryan were, "Don't you ever think of doing anything like this so fast! You're too young; you need time."

After a brief discussion of where we would live, Kevin moved into my house, avoiding a move or change in schools for Laura. Ryan graduated high school that year and moved into housing to attend OSU. Pete turned twenty-three the month Kevin and I married, and he had recently moved into an apartment near the OSU campus with his girlfriend and two dogs. Laura and Elizabeth were one year apart in school. Laura was nine and finishing the third grade in public school in Worthington; Elizabeth, a fourth-grader, would soon turn eleven. She attended a parochial school located midway between our home and her mother's. Laura would occasionally visit with her dad for an afternoon, maybe once a month or so, but Elizabeth was able to have a predictable schedule of weekends and one weekday with us, as well as vacations and time in the summer. Our life became a crescendo of family events, with music lessons, concerts, sports, and school functions.

Our families merged. If we had taken the metaphor of blending literally, then I would tell you we programmed the family blender to "fold," and in the gentlest way we knew, we became a family.

CHAPTER THIRTEEN

Winning the Adoption Lottery

Across the land, across the sea, there's a girl who's just like me.

She's got my eyes, she's got my chin.
Who could she be?
Of course! My Twin!

~ Laura Kathleen, age ten

In November 1993, a month before Laura's tenth birthday, I received a phone call from Jeff, a social worker with our adoption agency in Minnesota.

"I've been trying to reach you for several months," he told me. My remarriage and name change six months earlier had led to a delay in finding me. "We have some new information on your daughter. Are you interested in hearing it?"

"Oh, yes, of course," I responded, wondering what news there could be almost a decade after her adoption was complete.

"We received a letter from the birth mother in Seoul. It's written to 'the adoptive mother of SeonKyung Jung.'"

That's me, I thought, feeling breathless and confused. Although Laura strongly wished she would find her birth mother, I thought that was just a child's impossible dream, or a dream that would take years and years of searching to come true. Since there had been no identifying information on Laura's adoption papers sent by the Korean adoption agency and they had listed her parents as "unknown," I was shocked by this sudden turn of events.

"If you like, I can read it to you now," Jeff offered. "It was written in Korean, but one of our social workers translated it for us."

"I would love that!" My response was immediate. Would there be any reason not to hear it?

Jeff began:

Dear SeonKyung's adoptive mother,

How are you? I am feeling a kind of shameful to write to you. Nevertheless. I am starting this letter to say hello. It is already summer in Korea. You can tell it by looking at people's dress and by feeling temperature. How's the weather in United States?

I laughed to myself that she would be starting with talk of the weather. Korean etiquette? But it was now fall. She wrote this letter months ago!

I would like to say thank you for taking a good care of SeonKyung. I guess she is growing healthy. All family member here are doing fine. It is hard job to bring up children. I can imagine your difficulties very well. I really do respect you, SeonKyung's adoptive parents. It cannot be done without the love of Jesus. I am not entitled to say this, but still I do respect you and I will. In Korean age, SeonKyung will be fourth grade in elementary school. Time flies.

I chuckled at the American expression, time flies.

I do not know whether you are aware of it, but, actually SeonKyung is twin.

A twin? Unbelievable!

My heart was racing. How would I have known she was a twin?

A twin!

I had laughed at Laura thinking she could be a twin. Could she have sensed it somehow?

SeonKyung is elder and the one I have here is young sister. Also there is another baby sister.

This news was too much to take in!

A birth mother.

A twin.

And another sister?

I am really sorry for you, SeonKyung adoptive parents, even though I know it is asking too much, I really would like to get SeonKyung's picture. If you want, I will send our family picture to you next time.

Family? A birth father too?

I am sorry to ask your favor like this. I hope you can understand me.

Oh, I think I do understand you, Birth Mother. You want to see your daughter.

But don't feel sorry for *me*. For I am the lucky one!

I do not mean anything else. I just want to see how SeonKyung is now.

God bless you. Goodbye.
SeonKyung's birth mother.

The letter held news that was shocking. Hearing it left me numb and stunned. I asked Jeff to repeat parts of the letter. I scribbled, "Laura's a twin!" and "younger sister!" on a notepad next to my phone to keep my fingers busy. There's no way I would have forgotten it!

I didn't know the best way to present such information to a child, but one thing I was sure about: It was news I would need to share with Laura as soon as she arrived home from school that day.

I made a frenzied phone call to Kevin, telling him he must come home early from work. When Laura arrived home from school later that afternoon, I asked her to sit in the living room with us.

"I got a phone call today from the adoption agency in Minnesota." I tried to keep my voice steady. "They read a letter to me." Then taking a deep breath and making sure she was looking at me, I added, "It was from your birth mother."

"What?" she said, my words not yet fully registering.

"Your birth mother wrote a letter." This time, I said the words slowly, glancing at Kevin, who added, "The agency read the letter to your mom."

One second of recognition. Then an explosion of jubilation. A celebration. Jumping up and down and screaming, "My *birth* mother? *My* birth mother?"

"Laura, wait." I caught her arms mid-movement and turned her toward me. "There's one more thing." I could feel the energy in her arms, her eyes locked on mine. She stood motionless.

"Laura...you have a twin sister!"

Laura sat down. A wave of silence, then a wide smile washed over her face and seemed to spread to her toes. She beamed. "I knew I had a twin," she calmly and confidently stated. "Remember, Mom? I said that *maybe I have a twin?* I said that! And you said, 'Fat chance, Laura.'"

Suddenly Laura was in motion again. Dancing, leaping, and twirling in front of the window. For an instant, she became my three-year-old fairy princess again. This time, she didn't need the magic wand. I was ecstatic for her. I listened as she talked and exclaimed and shouted and yelled, while planning and scheming and plotting and designing her future.

That night, she danced up to her room as she headed for bed. Mixed into her running stream of conversation, I heard something about "winning the adoption lottery."

∾

In typical lottery-winning fashion, Laura experienced a strong initial euphoria.

Laura told her story to everyone she saw, including friends, teachers, and anyone else who'd listen. One of my former college roommates living in Cleveland told Laura's story to one of her friends employed by *The Cleveland Plain Dealer.* This led to our family being interviewed by one of their reporters and an article appearing on their front page on Christmas Day. "Mom's Letter Is Wish Come True for Girl," the headline read. News that Laura was a twin spread quickly. In January, Laura was interviewed and photographed for an article that appeared in *Woman's World* magazine.

Our family went through a whirlwind sharing of pictures and

letters between our family in Ohio and Laura's birth family in South Korea. We learned that Laura's birth mother, birth father, twin sister, younger sister, and paternal grandmother lived together in Seoul. The family ran and owned a restaurant.

Several months after she first heard from her birth family, Laura poured her heart out in a carefully crafted letter to her birth mother. It was important to her that her birth mother know she is happy.

"Dear Birth Mother,
...I understand why I was given up. I am thankful that I am not dead, because I would miss all the special moments that I have had. In my eyes, what you did for me is one of the most loving things a mother can do."

Ten-year-old logic, gratitude, and wisdom.

Then she wrote to her twin, waiting impatiently for responses, each letter sent and received requiring the additional step of translation through the adoption agency. Laura scrutinized the details in every received picture and pored over our family photos, selecting ones she believed gave the truest portrayal of our family.

These were happy and exciting years for Laura. Everything Laura did, she wanted it to be her best. If she were ever to meet her birth mother, Laura wanted her to be proud of her. When Laura was in third grade, she switched from piano lessons and started playing the violin. She wanted videos of her ice skating and playing the violin so she could send them to her birth family.

After a few years, we felt ready for a greater degree of openness and made the decision that our family would start to correspond directly with the birth family, no longer using our adoption agency to translate and shuffle our correspondence back and forth. The agency gave us the birth family's address and they received ours.

Laura had taken some Korean culture and language classes when she was younger, so I started talking with the people we had met there to help us with our search to find our own translator. We made friends with the Korean owners of a local dry-cleaning business, reached out to persons at the Korean Methodist church in Columbus, introduced ourselves to a university professor who was fluent in both Korean and English, and became friends with a Korean Ph.D. nursing student.

It was as if we had suddenly discovered a secret passage in our own backyard that opened on the other side of the world.

CHAPTER FOURTEEN

Incongruence

....

A mother understands what a child does not say.
~ Jewish proverb

....

As Laura approached her eleventh birthday, changes in her life picked up speed. Laura seemed resilient and to be adapting, but time would reveal that it was too much too fast.

Shortly after Kevin and I had married, Will and Irene divorced. Less than a year later, Will married Maureen, a woman he had met as students in a class at Ohio State. With Maureen's encouragement, Will expressed wanting to become more involved in Laura's life. For the first time ever, eleven-year-old Laura had a toothbrush and a room of her own at her father's house. With caution and guidance from psychologists, Laura slowly increased visitation time with Will and Maureen. For a few years, Laura would visit at their home one or two weekends a month. But as Laura became more involved with her friends and middle-school functions, she started to protest giving up her activities for time at her dad's.

Will responded to Laura's resistance and to my refusal to force her to visit with an unexpected court petition to change custody of Laura from me to him. Will wanted full custody of Laura! This shocked and alarmed me. I consulted an attorney. The court assigned Laura a guardian *ad litem* who met with her several times and visited with Laura in our home and in Will's home before representing her in court. The final decision by the judge stated "frequency and duration of visitation" for

Laura with her father would be totally at "Laura's initiation and discretion." Custody remained with me. These court decisions, along with an increase in the amount of child support he was required to pay, were a jolt to Will.

I believed the judge's visitation decision would feel empowering to Laura, now thirteen years old, but instead it confused her. She seemed to work even harder to please Will while fighting the guilt she felt over preferring to spend time with her friends rather than with him and Maureen. In addition, Laura had built an easy and strong relationship with Kevin, drawn by their similar interests in books and music. Kevin provided the piano accompaniment for violin recitals and competitions for Laura and some of her friends in the orchestra. But with Will's renewed interest, Laura was concerned about hurting her father's feelings, and she was confused by her own conflicting loyalties. Having the freedom to be in charge of her visitation schedule made her anxious, especially when discussing her plans with Will. I knew that interacting with Will could be challenging and intimidating. I monitored Laura closely and stepped in with suggestions when I felt she needed help, trying to keep enough distance so that any involvement from me would not trigger a challenging response from Will that would negatively affect Laura's internal conflicts.

Laura relied heavily on ice skating as an outlet for her physical and emotional energy. She had started skating when she was six years old. It came naturally to her and she appeared joyful when she skated around the rink, laughing, skating backward, or trying out new spins. Laura took group lessons, then private lessons from Don, a patient and kind, white-haired grandfather who would glide around the rink coaching her on her spins, humoring her when her perfectionism led to frustration. Don was a warm and comforting presence in Laura's life, and the Ohio State ice rink became a place for Laura to meet up with friends and make new ones.

One of the new "friends" she met was a man named Walter. Thin, agile, and an excellent skater, Walter appeared much younger than his forty-two years. Since I had returned to school for more advanced studies in nursing, I would study at the ice rink while Laura skated. Sitting in the bleacher section of the dilapidated old ice rink, keeping one eye on the little mice scurrying around beneath my feet, I was totally unaware of the havoc this friendly male would wreak on Laura. Clothed in a winter hat and gloves, clustered with eight, ten, or twelve middle and high school kids in the center of the rink, Walter appeared as one of them.

Walter was *not* one of them. He was evil. Without my awareness or suspicion, he befriended Laura, taught her ice skating skills, bought her hot chocolate, and even gave her a small necklace. Walter selected her, charmed her, groomed her, and when she was fourteen years old, he sexually abused her. By the time I became aware of what was happening, Walter had blurred Laura's sense of boundaries by building her trust, treating her specially, and getting her to believe that what he was doing wasn't monstrously wrong.

Walter would pick up Laura from school, take her to his house, and bring her home before my expected arrival from work, one hour after school was dismissed. One hour. How many times? I don't know. Maybe twice, three times, more? But one time I arrived home first. I saw Laura emerging from a car. I saw a man who looked like Walter from the ice rink driving the car. I watched Laura's goodbye to him as she hurried into our house. When the wave of realization of what could be going on rolled through me, it took all my strength not to vomit.

In those moments, did I do everything wrong? I didn't vomit, but I gagged. I screamed. I ranted. I raged. I paced. I cried hot and angry tears. I lost my mind. With only Laura and me in our home, she sat silently and watched her mother go insane.

After ninety seconds of me spewing all my emotions into the room, I stopped. *Laura needs me to be strong. Laura needs a mother, not a maniac.* I sat down beside Laura and put my arms around her.

"Yes," that was Walter, the guy from the skating rink.

"Yes," he brought her to his home. More than once.

And "yes" to the question I could barely force myself to ask that confirmed sexual acts.

Then Laura sat still and mute, casting her eyes down at her hands clutched tightly together in her lap, refusing to respond further to my barrage of questioning.

"I'm taking you to the emergency room," I firmly stated.

A quick glance at me, alarm in her eyes, she gazed back at her hands. "Okay, Mom," was her soft reply.

The detective in the emergency room was kind. Kind to me and to Laura. He talked with Laura alone shortly after our arrival. Then he talked with me while she was being examined. After he returned and talked with Laura a second time, trying to encourage her to press charges, he met with me again, saying, "She said she doesn't want to get him into trouble." The detective shared my frustration, both at her and at the law. "She's fourteen. If she were a few months younger, you as the mother could press charges, at least for interference with custody. But there is just not enough feedback coming from Laura to confirm

whys, the hows. *Why did you do this?* I wondered in the beginning, not in a judgmental way, but in a wanting-to-know-so-
I-could-fill-in-the-spaces kind of way. Was it lack of money or
fear of raising a child alone or just not wanting to be a mother?
How were you able to let a child go? I was bewildered when
I thought about anyone making a deliberate choice that could
permanently seal the deal on never seeing their child again. *Did
you miss her, your baby girl?*

My first thoughts and questions about Laura's birth mother
were based on assumptions drawn partially from an imagined
likely scenario and partially from words sent to us from the
Korean adoption agency. I assumed that the child profiled in
the packet sent to us was, like the majority of adoptees from
South Korea, a single birth from a young, unwed mother. "This
baby was found crying in front of the children's home by a staff
around 3 AM" and "with a slip of note, saying its birth date"
further influenced my belief that a single woman had given birth
to Laura. The statement under "Other information"—"Since
intake, there has been nobody to come see or inquire of her"—
convinced me that the mother had wanted to remain unknown.
I imagined a young woman whose life had been made easier
by placing her child for adoption, lifting the heavy burden of
stigma Koreans tend to place on unwed mothers.

I had mistakenly believed that the information sent to me
from the adoption agency in Seoul was not only the truth, but
the whole gospel truth. I never imagined the child I was adopting
was the older twin born to a securely married couple who had
joyfully welcomed two seemingly healthy girls into the world.

And what had Hyeja assumed about *me*, the woman who
was raising her child? What was she told when she and her

husband signed SeonKyung over to the Korean government, hoping their daughter's life would be saved in a country where she could receive the heart surgery they had been told she needed to survive? She knew from our letters that I had divorced and remarried. Would that affect what she thought of me? How will she respond when she learns that Laura never had, nor even needed, heart surgery?

In the beginning, Laura's birth mother was not even a name on a page. I never imagined that someday she would be visiting in our home. But four years and eight months after receiving the first letter, Hyeja and EunKyung arrived at the Columbus International Airport to spend three weeks with Laura, Kevin, and me in our home. Aun, my South Korean friend, was with us at the airport. Aun was excited and eager to meet Hyeja and EunKyung and to translate during their visit.

I will always remember watching Laura as she stood waiting at the arrival gate: dressed in summer shorts, tank top, and sandals, clutching a bouquet of daisies and wildflowers; pacing back and forth, straining to see more of the passengers who were filing through the gate, her shiny black ponytail bobbing side to side. As the last few passengers emerged, she spotted EunKyung. Although not an identical twin, she was easily recognized. EunKyung was wearing a backpack, smiling, and guiding her mother, almost dragging her forward. Laura walked toward them with arms open. She and EunKyung embraced, laughing. Laura unwrapped her arms, turned, and handed the flowers to her birth mother, who grabbed Laura and held on tight. The sight of Laura, at the center of a trio of small Asian females, held in the grip of a sobbing woman—whose face, tear-stained and open-mouthed in a rictus of agony and joy—is forever imprinted in my mind.

I wasn't sure what I was supposed to be feeling, but I was mostly bathed in feelings of contentment and relief that the long-awaited moment had finally arrived. I watched Laura's immersion in the moment. Joy permeated her laughter. Her pleasure was palpable. I looked around and saw a small group of people yet to leave the gate. They stood and watched our group, commenting softly to each other. I wondered what they were thinking. Surely they must have quickly recognized that a much-anticipated reunion was happening. I was relieved when they moved on, glad that the gate was at the end of the terminal and that the airport was not very busy. This reunion felt intimate to me. I didn't want anyone else peeking at my daughter's moment.

After a few minutes of hugs to Kevin and me from EunKyung, and awkward hugs and bows between Hyeja and me and Kevin, Aun introduced herself to Laura's birth mother and sister and helped to get the procession started, shuffling off to the baggage claim. And it *was* a procession, with Hyeja not willing to detach herself from Laura's arm, and EunKyung supporting her mother's other side. As the attached trio moved along, with some bumbling and stumbling, it occurred to me that this was the way they had started out. They were once one body, a maternal-child unit. Hyeja had been the nurturer and protector for nine months while Laura and EunKyung developed and grew, held tight, arms and legs intertwined, hearing the beating of their mother's heart.

We learned that Hyeja had been in an auto accident requiring surgery on her leg a few months before she was scheduled to leave for the U.S. She had a limp and walked as though in pain, relying on a cane. Yet she was constantly smiling, tears flowing down her cheeks. She was determined not to miss this trip. Nothing would keep her from seeing her daughter again.

Prior to their visit, friends wondered whether it would be difficult to watch my daughter with her birth mother. Much to their surprise, I did not feel threatened by Laura's quest to meet and know her birth family. Most importantly, I knew the relationship Laura and I had was solid. Connecting with her birth family, in my mind, would only strengthen our relationship, not weaken it. Why would seeing my daughter happy be difficult for me? What I did feel, though, was a conflict between my wanting to help Laura complete her desired connection with her birth family and my wanting to protect her emotionally and psychologically. Laura had been through a difficult year, and I didn't want her hurt again. But when the opportunity presented itself that her birth mother and twin could visit us in our home, I did what I could to make it happen. I was an accomplice in connecting Laura with her birth family.

The visit did take more emotional energy than I had expected, but that was related to watching and listening to Laura as she shared her feelings with me. We had a moment in the car alone one day, driving slowly through our residential area, running some errands. "I love my birth mother because she is my birth mother," she started out, "but I really don't *like* her very much."

I stayed quiet, giving Laura space to explain. Laura's birth mother often hovered over her, sometimes touching her face or adjusting her clothing or trying to cover her bare arms and shoulders if she was wearing a tank top. Usually these actions were accompanied by short giggles and a smile. Most of the things that Laura didn't "like" were Birth Mother's attempts to *mother* her.

"*You're* my mom," Laura said as I pulled into a parking spot. Turning toward her, I realized she had been fighting back tears and the tears had won, spilling over her cheeks as she muttered, "I'm worried that maybe you don't love me as much as you used to. You're so willing to share me with her."

This was a twist I hadn't expected. I had been trying to stand back and let their relationship develop without my interference. I did have my moments when I looked forward eagerly to the drive to the airport for Hyeja and EunKyung's return trip home. Sharing my daughter did get frustrating and annoying, but I reminded myself that three weeks was a very brief period in Laura's life. I must have hidden these moments too well from Laura, for my relaxed attitude came across as uncaring to her.

"I love you more than anything and couldn't possibly love you more, Laura," I said, now wiping tears from my eyes. "You will always be my daughter. I will always be your mother. Forever. I just want you to be happy."

We hugged as we laughed, then cried a little more before finishing our errands and heading home.

After dinner on the final night of their visit, we sat around the table talking, with Aun translating. The girls eventually wandered off to their own fun, and Hyeja and I were able to share our thoughts. She was "so sorry" about my son who had died. It had been mentioned in one of our letters to her. Even with the struggle to communicate between two languages, we could talk mother to mother. Her "so sorry" felt genuine. I knew that only a few years earlier, she had thought she would never see her daughter again. She had gone for ten years not knowing whether her daughter was dead or alive. It was a heartache for her, not knowing where SeonKyung was.

I had not yet experienced the heartache of not knowing where my child was, of not knowing if she was even alive. I believed I knew where Shawn was. It was the *missing him* that was painful. Hyeja had endured both the missing and the not knowing about her daughter.

By the end of the evening, we both knew this trip had been a gift for both of us. For her, it was seeing, hearing, and touching her daughter again. For me, the gift was seeing my daughter's dream come true.

Though Hyeja had found her daughter and had seen that her daughter was alive and happy, she would have to say goodbye again. When you add a tincture of her Korean shame to the mix—"*I am feeling a kind of shameful to write to you*"—and her yearning to know how her daughter was doing—"*I do not mean anything else. I just want to see how SeonKyung is now*"—it was easy to appreciate the emotional roller coaster the visit had been for her.

Laura had yearned for this birth-family connection ever since she was old enough to understand that there was another mother, a birth mother. But by the time they reconnected, it was the meeting up and getting to know EunKyung that gave Laura the most joy.

Laura and EunKyung met when they were approaching fifteen, that age when profound developmental emotional shifts occur no matter where a girl is growing up. They filled up each other's spaces of loneliness and sense of isolation and need to have a best friend. The time they spent together was magical. EunKyung knew some beginning English, but this was her first exposure to having to speak it and be understood all the time. In spite of that, she and Laura clicked from the second they saw each other at the airport. For three weeks they were almost inseparable. When I looked out the kitchen window, I could see them skipping up the street, arms wrapped around each other, singing, talking, or laughing. Giggles could be heard throughout the house when they were making videos. In one video, they are singing "Twinkle, Twinkle, Little Star" together, Laura in English and EunKyung in Korean. When Laura told EunKyung that she had been named after another Laura, a friend of Ryan's who has a twin sister named Lisa, they decided that EunKyung's American name would be Lisa.

Laura was finally walking arm in arm, talking, singing, and laughing with the girl from "across the sea" whom she wrote about when she was ten years old. No, they were not identical. But she had her eyes. She had her chin.

"Who could she be?"

Of course, her twin.

CHAPTER SIXTEEN

Who Are You?

Who in the world am I? Ah, that's the great puzzle.
~ Lewis Carroll, *Alice's Adventures in Wonderland*

Was Laura at a good age to connect with her birth mother that summer when she was fourteen? I'm not sure. Did I make the right decision at the right time for my daughter? I don't know. I certainly thought so at the time. It was something she had wanted so badly.

But the fall after her birth family's visit, Laura started high school, and dark clouds of negativity rolled in. In December, Laura turned fifteen. She became more self-critical and despondent, with those clouds of negativity increasing in intensity and frequency. "I had a horrible day today," Laura would announce as she slumped into the house after school, head down, dragging her backpack or violin case. Upon questioning, she would tell about a teacher who had raised an eyebrow at her, or a grade of B when she had expected an A, or her inability to perfect her spin on her ice skates. Events were viewed as black or white, okay or terrible, ecstatic or depressing. Her happy, positive switch had no dimmer; it was either fully on or off. One event that she perceived as negative colored her entire day. In reality, her grades did begin to slip. At first, it was almost imperceptible, an A- when she was used to an A, then a B in place of the A-.

More significant was the gradual shift in how she viewed the world, which included how she viewed her own genesis. Before Laura had met her birth mother, she often explained to people that her birth mother placed her for adoption because of Laura's heart defect. She would always add, "She loved me so much, she gave me life twice." After her birth mother visited, Laura developed a different perspective. She was disappointed by her birth mother. Laura's explanation: "I just thought she'd be more like you, Mom."

Laura started to focus on her own imperfections, and she began right at the heart of the matter. It seemed that her fifteen-year-old logic, or not-so-logical logic, went like this:

I was born with a hole in my heart. It is called a ventricular septal defect. Therefore, I am defective. My birth parents couldn't afford to have it fixed, so they gave me up, thinking it would help me survive. If I, Laura, had not been born defective, I would not have been given up.

Not that she wished she had grown up in Korea. "No way. Never!" she said. She didn't even want to visit Korea. She just didn't like being "defective." And another question now added to her torment: "Why did they have another baby? If they couldn't take care of me, why did they think they could take care of another baby?" She felt she had been replaced by her younger sister, EunSeon, who, as far as we knew, was not defective.

Laura had continued in regular therapy after the experience with Walter. That fall she was referred to a psychiatrist who started Laura on an antidepressant. Some days were good and some were not. There was not a consistent pattern, so it was difficult to tell if the medication was of any help. My years of working on a child psychiatric unit gave me more knowledge, but Laura was *my* child. I lost most of my ability to be objective.

It was as though a reverse magnet had taken control of my daughter. She went from a happy, optimistic, wanting-to-tell-me-everything child, to a sulky, moody young girl who pulled away from me. I had mothered two sons through the teen years, so yes, I knew. All teens pull away. But not like Laura.

Laura didn't just pull away. She began to run away.

Often and far, fleeing from the house in the middle of the night, shinnying down a bed sheet from her second-story window, hightailing it to places unknown, and disappearing in ways I've buried too deeply to recall.

At first there were short episodes of her disappearing for a few hours, not being where she was supposed to be when I picked her up, not showing up at her orchestra rehearsal, leaving school before her last class. Atypical and unusual behavior for Laura.

Her first overnight running episode took place over a three-day period on a hot weekend in June, the summer after her birth mother's visit. Her depression had been building. Leading up to that weekend, Laura was sulky and irritable but had also shown spurts of energy and excitement. She didn't seem to sleep much but was up each morning without a struggle.

On Friday evening, after I drove her and a girlfriend to a movie, she was nowhere to be found when it was time for her friend's parents to pick them up. The weekend consisted of frantic phone calls, messages, and calls from friends, and finally a solid reconnection on Sunday afternoon when her friend's older boyfriend drove her home. She had no explanation that could account for the almost three days of meandering. She was tearful, agitated, and depressed. Her adventure landed her in an urgent care psychiatric clinic.

"I know she says she's not suicidal," I told the soft-spoken, attentive Dr. Bergren when it was my turn in his office after he had interviewed Laura. "But if this whirlwind she's on doesn't stop, I'm afraid she's going to kill herself!"

If I appeared on the outside as I felt on the inside, then Dr. Bergren was viewing a crazed woman. I couldn't sleep, I couldn't eat, and I didn't give a shit what I looked like. All I could do was cry or struggle not to cry. I feared Laura's behaviors were going to get her killed, she was not going to survive another week, and then I would be grieving the loss of another child. Any thought of life without Laura was unimaginable.

"Let's see if we can get her hospitalized. She'll be safe there and it will give us a chance to get a correct diagnosis," Dr. Bergren advised. I wanted to hug him. When he added, "With all the agitation and anxiety she has, I suspect she may have a bipolar type of depression," the relief I felt was almost euphoric. To me, a diagnosis meant a plan and treatment and safety.

I credit Dr. Bergren with saving my daughter's life. At least for saving her life *that* day, after the most dramatic and colossal go-round of her depression to date.

Although Laura later reported only foggy recall of Dr. Bergren and his arranging for her hospitalization, she and I both remembered Dr. Kline, her attending psychiatrist during her inpatient hospital stay. Dr. Kline, the director of the adolescent unit, was a fifty-ish, rotund man with a gregarious smile, big, dark eyes, and a Santa Claus chuckle. When he spoke, his words flowed with a Southern drawl, deep and silky, drawing people into whatever he was saying. He certainly drew me in as he sat directly across from Kevin and me at Laura's discharge conference. He, together with a psychiatric nurse, the unit social worker, the psych resident, and a baby-faced medical student had teamed up to review Laura's hospital stay with us.

"I'm just a defective throwaway," was what Dr. Kline reported Laura saying to him, words dramatized with the wave of his hand with its eye-catching, ring-adorned pinkie finger. Stabbing words that hurt my heart.

I don't know what it felt like to be Laura in Dr. Kline's therapy office, but it must have made her feel safe enough to talk, to open up, and to share the pain that had led her to him. I tried to imagine myself as fifteen-year-old Laura sitting in a small room face-to-face with Dr. Kline. "What's it like to be you today, Laura? Tell me what brought you here." Perhaps it was his large, soft presence or his kindness or his we-have-all-day-here-'cause-I'm-not-goin'-nowhere manner that put her at ease. I really didn't care what it was. I was just grateful it was happening and hopeful it would make life better.

We had ridden one huge wave of Laura being down in the dumps and her attempting to cope by running. We all had made it through an episode of Laura being missing. We had called the local police; we had registered her with the National Center for Missing & Exploited Children (NCMEC), a nonprofit organization to help find missing children and prevent child victimization; and we had engaged family and friends in her search. When she was found, we took her to mental health emergency care. She was hospitalized, evaluated, tested, medicated, and set free with a page of discharge plans.

"You're never happier than your unhappiest child," a therapist-colleague once said, sharing his wisdom on parenthood. As I sat in the conference room listening to Dr. Kline and his punctuated words, I couldn't remember happy. The adventures of the past year had depleted my supply of happy. And I wondered again why *I* was not able to fix things for Laura.

Taking Laura home from the hospital after her discharge conference, I felt like a survivor. But it was not over. In fact, it was only the beginning; we had had just a taste of what was in store for her and our family over the next two years. The running episodes that led to Dr. Bergren, Dr. Kline, and Laura's inpatient hospital stay were a preview of the nightmare we were soon to experience.

Laura was just at the beginning of her long and meandering path of exploration to find an answer to *Who in the world am I?*

Like Alice, Laura had fallen down the rabbit hole.

CHAPTER SEVENTEEN

Balancing Act

In Western society, Yin-Yang is often referred to as "Yin and Yang" and brings to mind simple contrasts such as dark and light...But Yin-Yang is much more than mere opposites. Rather, it represents the idea that the interaction of contradictory forces not only creates harmony, but also makes for a greater, more complete "whole."

~ Rebecca Shambaugh

In late June of 1999, Laura was released from the University Medical Center Hospital on two medications, an antidepressant along with Lithium, added for its mood-stabilizing and anti-suicidal properties. Lithium calmed her. No. It blanketed her. Smothered her and stole her spirit and her sparkle. And made her pee more. She hated taking it. It did help her anxiety, but as the anxiety dissipated, depression rose to the surface.

Laura returned to high school in the fall and started her sophomore year at the Linworth campus, an alternative high school in Worthington. The purpose of the Linworth Alternative Program is to enable students to more fully engage in their education by allowing them to make more choices and by placing them in situations requiring higher levels of responsibility. It focuses on independence and experiential education, appealing to the bright, inquisitive, and creative student—the student Laura had been in middle school.

Laura had always been an excellent and enthusiastic student with a bent toward perfectionism. As a sophomore, she spent most of the day at the Linworth campus, except when she would be bused to the main Worthington High School campus for orchestra and an occasional "main-campus-only" class. She resumed her ice skating, but with less passion, less frequency, more supervision, and at a different rink from where she had met Walter. She performed as a violinist in the Columbus Cadet Symphony Orchestra. Her depression abated as the Christmas holidays approached, giving all of us a feeling of hope as January and the new year were about to start.

Spring and the end of her sophomore year of high school brought another swing in Laura's mood. She had increased energy but poor focus on her school work, resulting in needing an extension into the summer to complete work in a math class. Some days she would be exhilarated and optimistic, but a few days later, anxious and irritable with little desire for sleep. She was taken off her Lithium due to side effects and her unwillingness to continue it. But she remained on her antidepressant, Prozac, and started a different mood stabilizer, Neurontin.

⚬⚬

Laura would often retreat to her bedroom, amidst her books and journals, her head resting beneath a yin-yang tapestry hanging on her wall. Laura had accumulated several forms of the yin-yang symbol, from wall hangings to drawings to jewelry.

In Chinese philosophy, the yin-yang describes how opposite forces are complementary and interdependent, each containing part of the other. The yin-yang symbol usually shows a circle equally divided into black and white sections by a reverse S-like shape. Each side contains part of the other, with yin being black with the white dot of yang and yang being white with the black dot of yin. It was easy to see Laura's moods in relation to the yin-yang, opposite forces that were interconnected.

Yin is soft, yielding, diffuse, hidden, covert, passive, water, earth, moon, the north side of the mountain, and the south bank of the river. Yang is hard, solid, focused, open, overt, active, fire, sky, sun, the south side of the mountain, and the north bank of the river. Sunlight plays over a mountain and a shady place is occluded by the mountain's height. As the sun moves across the sky, the two sides trade places with each other, opening up what was hidden and yielding to what was solid. The outer circle represents everything in the universe existing together. The yin-yang symbolizes the seeking of vision. To have vision, to see where you are going, you must have balance.

Even though I had worked in the mental health field for much of my nursing career, and this was my second year working as a nurse practitioner and clinical nurse specialist at a downtown community mental health center, I was slow to absorb and process that Laura's moods were consistent with the seasonal pattern of spring and summer highs and winter lows commonly seen in persons with bipolar depression.

My work at Southeast Mental Health Center focused on the physical health needs, such as hypertension, diabetes, asthma, and chronic obstructive pulmonary disease, of the severely mentally ill: the homeless, persons with alcohol or drug addictions, those suffering from a psychosis or dementia, or persons experiencing severe depression or anxiety. One day I drove home from work distressed about the depressed and anxious woman who had come to my clinic with her hand wrapped in white bread to keep it clean after her husband had bitten her, removing a huge chunk of flesh from her hand. Another day I drove home smiling about the seventy-year-old man who appeared at the door of my small office stark naked, fondling his privates, trying to communicate to me that he was frustrated with an annoying crotch itch from a yeast infection. My lady with the bread on her wound and my elderly naked man, *they* were mentally ill. *They* had a mental disorder. I preferred thinking of Laura's moods as resembling those contained in the circle of a yin-yang: complementary and interdependent. Not *disordered*.

Reflecting on those years, I view myself as having accepted the highs and lows of Laura's moods as a shadow of bipolar disorder. A mere shadow of a mental health concern—possibly cast by the adolescent years—that certainly needed to be treated and dealt with, but a shadow that would pass over her. It would eventually go away. The sun would come out, and Laura, true to the meaning of her Korean birth name, would be consistently "bright and good-natured" again. How much of what Laura was expressing was related to her early beginnings of being separated from her twin, or having four different primary caregivers in the first fifteen months of her life, or her relationship with Will, or the trauma from Walter, or meeting her birth mother, or the developing connections with her birth culture?

I was hesitant to lean on Kevin, for he too was confused and befuddled by everything to which Laura was reacting. Elizabeth was nearing her senior year in high school, playing on the drumline in the marching band and thinking about life after high school. She needed Kevin's focus on her. And what would I do if Kevin viewed decisions regarding Laura differently from the way I viewed them? Laura was *my* daughter. I loved her and knew her better than anyone else did.

At the core of it all was my trying to figure out what was best for Laura. What was helping? What was making it worse? What actions were enhancing my daughter's life? Was I, in any way, an accomplice to her misery? Was I doing the right thing as each crisis hit, one after another?

There were too many moments when I felt as if I were alone in the ocean. In a storm. At first fighting each wave, but then learning to ride the waves and becoming part of them as they took me surging up and then crashing down, almost believing the waves and I were one.

I was fighting hard not to lose my balance.

CHAPTER EIGHTEEN

On the Lam

I guess that's the really nice thing about disappearing: the part where people look for you and beg you to come home.

~ Lauren Oliver, *Vanishing Girls*

That summer of 2000, after her sophomore year, Laura begged to have her twin sister come and visit her again. To my surprise, Laura's birth family agreed, and EunKyung arrived in July for a three-week stay. Certainly, *this* visit would boost Laura's mood.

The twins were now sixteen and Laura had her driver's license, although I usually drove them wherever they needed to go. Just as during the first visit, Laura and EunKyung went everywhere together. Tightly knit, they walked arm in arm around the neighborhood, laughed and cooked together in the kitchen, or sat on Laura's bed late at night—cross-legged, heads touching, whispery voices—sharing secrets only twins would understand. Laura had grown up with two protective brothers, Ryan, ten years older, and Pete, fifteen years older. When Laura was nine, she was excited that Elizabeth, a year and a half older, became her stepsister. But being with her twin was different.

Laura and EunKyung spent more time with Laura's friends than with family. This was different from the visit when they were fourteen and Laura's birth mother was with us. EunKyung slid right into the circle of Laura's friends, which had expanded at the unique opportunity of getting to know Laura's twin. They went to movies in groups of four, six, or more. They shared a more intense interest in boys and makeup and fashion and current music and movies. When we entered Blockbuster to rent some videos, EunKyung swooned at the sight of a huge poster, placed her hands over her heart, then opened her arms wide saying, "Oh, Leonardo DiCaprio, I l-o-v-e you!" Leonardo stood seven feet tall on the Titanic, reaching his arms toward those who entered the store. He stared right into EunKyung's dark, almond-shaped eyes.

Two weeks into EunKyung's visit, I awoke on a Saturday morning to a quiet house. I assumed the girls were sleeping in.

"Is Laura coming down for breakfast?" My question received a muffled response from EunKyung as she quietly padded down the stairs after emerging from the upstairs bedroom. I brushed it off, needing to head upstairs myself. I looked into the room where Laura and EunKyung had been sleeping. There was no Laura. No Laura in either of the other two bedrooms. No Laura in either bathroom. My heart did a flip.

"EunKyung? Where's Laura?" I tried to hide the dread that hung heavily in my chest.

"Uh…Laura? Uh…don't know." She said with a shrug of her shoulders, eyes open wide.

"What do you mean, you *don't know*?" I asked, louder and sharper, panic permeating my voice.

"Don't know," EunKyung repeated, shrugging her shoulders again, casting her eyes downward.

Kevin went to the garage, car keys in hand, intending to go to the barber and run some errands, but abruptly barged back inside.

The adjuster paused, looking up from his paperwork to meet my eyes. "No. Why would they do that?"

"Why *wouldn't* they do that?" I asked. *Shit, if the car looks like this, what did Laura look like? If the car had met such destruction, wasn't anyone else except Kevin and me panicked about the state of Laura?*

I explained that my daughter, who had been driving the car, was still missing. The adjuster had no answer for me. He was too involved with the numbers, trying to determine if the car should be totaled or repaired. Or maybe he found it more pleasant to look at the numbers on his page rather than the agony on my face. He wasn't expected to have the expertise to deal with the parent of a missing teen. I wondered if he had a teenage daughter at home.

The way he treated me had a familiar feel—similar to the way some had treated me after Shawn died—as if I had something contagious. *Stand too close to me and you might "catch" being the parent of a dead child*, it had been in the past. Now it's *Look into my eyes and I might infect you with my "I am the parent-of-a-missing-teen" status.*

Kevin and I busied ourselves with work, heading out each morning in different directions, me going south to downtown in my purple Mazda and Kevin driving west in the Enterprise rental of the week. The decision of our insurance company not to total Kevin's car resulted in several more weeks of repair work. One evening as were we returning from one of our numerous trips to the shop for updates, we pulled into the parking lot of our neighborhood grocery store. It was just before 10 p.m. on the twenty-first day without Laura. My cell phone rang.

The caller identified himself as a police officer. He wanted to verify whether I was the mother of the missing teenager from

Worthington, Ohio. He had identified her from the poster from the NCMEC that hung in his station.

"Ma'am, I believe the girl we have here in Cleveland is your daughter. She's okay, but she won't tell us her real name."

I gasped, barely able to breathe. And I was stunned when I realized he meant Cleveland, Ohio, and not Cleveland Avenue, a main street running north and south through Columbus. Laura was 150 miles away in East Cleveland. She had no car, only the clothes on her back, and a pair of flip-flops on her feet. *How in the hell did she get there?*

We drove straight to the police station in East Cleveland, more than a three-hour drive, arriving close to 2 a.m. The station was dark, old, and dirty and was located in a high-crime area. It was even more frightful when seen through my sleep-deprived eyes in the middle of the night.

"We saw this white child being pushed out of a slowly moving car and we knew she didn't belong here," the officers explained as I sat in the station with my arm around Laura. She was thin and dirty. Her feet had bloody scabs caused by the burlap straps of her flip-flops cutting into her feet.

My spirited, pampered, cherished daughter disguised as a despondent, underfed, neglected little street urchin.

My "white child" had stayed in a predominantly black area, she later explained, because she felt *protected*. People looked out for her in the ghetto on the East side of Cleveland. They told her she looked out of place, cautioned her to be careful, and gave her quarters to call for a ride or a dollar to get a sandwich.

Childproof locks in place, I sat with her in the back seat. Laura laid her head on my lap and cried. "Mom, I've been through hell. I'm so sorry."

I cried, too, and kissed her over and over, hugging her tightly, every nerve in my body hypervigilant and on guard. Certainly she couldn't slip from my grasp on the way home. I asked no questions. And I had plenty of questions, but part of me didn't want to know the answers. At least, not then. She was safe. She was alive. She was still Laura. I wanted only to bask in the warmth of the moment and hold on.

In the weeks ahead, I would learn some of what had happened to her while she was gone. I would learn of the places she'd been, how she traveled, who took her there, who fed her, where she slept—but I never learned everything I wanted to know. There were missing pieces, partly because Laura wouldn't say, but mostly because Laura couldn't remember. Years later, she would marvel at all she couldn't recall.

Exhausted and bleary-eyed, Kevin glanced frequently in his rear-view mirror at two of the people he deeply loved—such a strange and increasingly unrecognizable mother-daughter duo. He quietly drove us home.

∾

Laura had her first visit with her new psychiatrist, Dr. Carol, a few days later. She had been on a waiting list for months to see Dr. Carol, a well-respected physician whose specialty was working with teens with mood disorders. Since Laura had been wandering around for several weeks, she had not been taking any medication. Dr. Carol had her resume both her medications and talked about possible changes to consider in the future. With only a few weeks of summer remaining before school was to start, she asked Laura to come back in two weeks.

Laura continued to communicate with EunKyung as summer turned to fall, but I stopped sending any letters to Korea. I let any communication with the birth family stagnate. What did they know about Laura's adventure? What did EunKyung tell them when she returned home? What did they understand about Laura or about mental illness, still a taboo subject in Korea? My emotions, contaminated by physical and mental exhaustion, were a mix of anger, fear, and not really caring about what was going on with Laura's birth family. I wanted only for my daughter to be safe. And sane.

I didn't care if we heard from anyone in Korea ever again.

CHAPTER NINETEEN

Contain and Protect

And though she be but little, she is fierce.
~ William Shakespeare, *A Midsummer Night's Dream*

Retrieving Laura from the bowels of East Cleveland necessitated other changes besides a new psychiatrist. Kevin and I decided it would be good to install an alarm system in our home. Something more than bugging her room with the baby monitor I had hidden under her bed. Safer than the fire hazard of removing the latches from her bedroom windows to keep them permanently locked.

"Ma'am, you sure you want this system installed this way? If I set it up like this, your alarm's gonna go off when people *leave* this house, not when they break in."

"Right," I responded stone-faced. I wanted to tell him I didn't understand how my life had changed so much that I had to lock my child *inside*.

I also believed Laura needed a change of school. Even Laura agreed that she no longer fit in at Linworth, where freedom to make choices required an ability to manage higher levels of responsibility. For weeks after returning home, she felt shame about her fleeing in the middle of the night. "I thought of no one but myself," she stated later, awareness creeping in.

Kevin and I looked at private schools, believing that might help. Laura went along with the decision and passively complied with being enrolled in Village Academy, a small, elite, and *expensive* private school in Powell, a quaint Ohio city located northwest of our home in Worthington. Academically it was a perfect fit for our bright, articulate, athletic daughter. I flirted briefly with a vision of Laura excelling academically, playing on the lacrosse team, blending in with her peers, sitting first-chair violin in the orchestra, and beginning and ending each day dressed in her school uniform and a happy smile. Except for the school uniform, Laura had been all of that in the past, and more. I did not verbalize my fantasy to Laura, but I'm sure she sensed my wishes and my worry about her future. After signing the school's financial contract—a nine-month commitment of payments—and plunking down a huge amount of cash, I set my morning alarm extra early for the twenty-minute school commute. I prayed for Laura's survival and my sanity.

September was a good month. Kevin and I got into a routine of transporting Laura to and from school each day. My work at the community mental health agency was gratifying and gave me flexibility. Laura found the classes at Village Academy fun and stimulating. She started a job at Wendy's, located a short walk from the Linworth campus where she had previously gone to school.

Laura's mood was upbeat, almost euphoric at times. She had more energy. After seeing her so depressed, I viewed it as a hopeful sign. But there were times I was a bit concerned: once when her school reported that she, like Houdini, would disappear and then reappear throughout the day, and again when she took off her sweater after I picked her up from school one day and both her arms were covered with watches. Six or seven Rolex watches she had asked to "borrow" from the students in her class.

"Laura, what the heck is that?" I had asked, surprised and alarmed. "You have to make sure everyone gets those back tomorrow. It's not normal to do that, Laura. And it's not funny."

"Mom, I didn't steal them. They gave them to me. They're all rich there. All the kids drive Beamers," was her explanation. "They trust me, Mom."

Kevin or I would drop her off and pick her up from work at Wendy's. But one Sunday afternoon we agreed with her request that she drive herself. After more than six weeks of Laura doing well in her classes and being responsible at her job, it seemed like a safe thing to do, a step in lengthening the leash that tethered her to home. To me. Later that afternoon, I suggested to Kevin we go to Wendy's for some chili.

"It can be a surprise," I had suggested.

I didn't spot my car as we pulled into the Wendy's parking lot. Thinking she may have gone home early, I headed inside to check. My heart sank when I was told, "Laura didn't come to work today."

Getting no response from Laura's cell phone, Kevin and I headed home, called the local police, and filled out the necessary missing-child paperwork. Laura driving my uniquely colored, purple Mazda MX-3 was an asset in finding her. On Wednesday, three days later, she was picked up by the Ohio State Highway Patrol, driving south on I-71 at eighty-five miles per hour with another teenager, Carla Losey, a girl two years older who had more freedom and street smarts than Laura. Since Laura had been registered as a missing teen, the car was impounded. The highway patrolman could have had us pick her up, but he found her engaging and told us he'd meet us at the Columbus Police Station. He drove her the forty miles to downtown Columbus himself.

"She's a fascinating young lady," he said. "She told me all about her adoption story, being a twin and all. I told her she's a lucky girl." He was the father of two young adopted sons.

Her passenger would not be as lucky. Laura would not keep a connection with Carla. But we did learn through our local news two years later that, on New Year's Eve, Carla made her final disappearance. She became frozen in time, her pretty, twenty-year-old face staring out from missing-person posters.

A decade later, we learned of a $100,000 reward for information leading to the arrest or indictment of persons involved in Carla's disappearance. Laura believed Carla had been killed. "She hung around with dangerous characters." Some of whom, I surmised, Laura had also met.

The day after we picked up Laura from the state highway patrolman, Kevin, Laura, and I drove the forty minutes to the impound lot to pick up my car. My mind and body had experienced every emotion imaginable in the twenty-four hours since Laura had been handed back to us. I had been flooded initially with intense relief that she was safe, relief that shook my insides and spilled tears from my eyes. But relief was followed by anger, the kind of anger you feel when your two-year-old darts in front of a car to retrieve a toy: a frantic, lunatic anger where you want to shake them and squeeze them and pull their hair while hugging and smothering them with kisses and screams. Of course, there was that fear it would happen again. I wanted to chain Laura to my wrist and put her legs in shackles.

Laura witnessed my tears, but I reined in my anger and fear, focusing instead on a prevention plan. Laura had an appointment with Dr. Carol on Friday, and I was clinging to hope that she would provide the counsel and advice Laura needed.

After leaving the impound lot, we stopped for dinner at an Amish restaurant. It felt like a normal thing to do. I craved normal. And to anyone glancing at us as we ate, I'm sure we appeared to be content with each other. It was a beautiful October night, with a full harvest moon filling the sky on the eve of Friday the Thirteenth, 2000. I realized also that Laura was premenstrual, something I had learned to keep track of on my hypervigilant-mother calendar. I told my mind to downplay any significance of the full moon, premenstrual body, and Laura's building euphoria.

With Kevin following behind me, I drove my car home, wrapped securely in its solid frame and the warmth and mystery of its purple color. I merged onto the freeway and shifted into high gear, leaving the Amish cornfields behind. As Laura sat next to me, I thought about her hand and how it had grasped the gear shift forty-eight hours earlier as she had sped away from home. Now, with Laura safe and happily chatting away in the passenger seat, both our bodies full of wholesome food and Amish simplicity, I could feel my spirit and hope rising. The moon eclipsed my yesterday's fear as I rode the wave upward, fighting the urge to let my spirit soar.

Arriving home, I locked all the doors and windows, secured the reverse-installed alarm, and turned on the computer in our lower-level family room to check my email. Laura came down the stairs.

"G'night, Mom, I'm heading to bed," she said sweetly, placing her hand on my shoulder as she kissed my cheek. Her long, black hair brushed against my face. "Thanks for helping me out today. Love you."

I stood up by my desk and watched as she quickly ran up the family room stairs. Laura seemed happy, her face radiant. *In less than twelve hours, we will be sitting in Dr. Carol's office,* I thought to myself. *She will help us make a plan.* I breathed more deeply and turned back to close down my computer for the night.

Less than a minute later, I heard a crash. Calling up to Laura got no response. Running upstairs, I felt a breeze. Saw the screen from the 14-inch-wide kitchen window on the floor.

Laura had loosened the kitchen window screen with her still-child-sized hands and slid her tiny frame through the narrow opening of the only window in our home not connected to our alarm.

Laura. Gone. The eve of Friday the Thirteenth. A full moon. No phone. No purple Mazda to help track her down. Only an hour earlier, she had sat next to me, happily chatting away as we drove home, that huge full moon lighting up the sky.

But what was she fleeing from this time? Any of the times? Did Laura even know? The urge to flee, to take flight, is one symptom that makes bipolar depression different from plain depression or unipolar depression. It is difficult for people to understand, and it is difficult to treat. A person with bipolar depression would tell you that taking flight is not necessarily a good feeling. It can be like the irresistible urge to scratch an itch. It should feel good, but it doesn't. It doesn't fix the problem and it often makes it worse, leaving scars. Some people label the fight or flight that comes with the depression of having bipolar disorder as "hypomania." But it has been described by some who have experienced it as a miserable, menacing mania laced with anxiety.

Yes, this running episode was different. I knew it. Laura was not depressed like she was before her first hospitalization when she had met Dr. Bergren. She was not in a panic as she surely must have been when she and EunKyung made their Steak 'n Shake escape and crashed Kevin's car. This episode had no identifying trigger. It felt like a spontaneous creation that had emerged from rapidly moving brain cells, with a DiCaprio *Catch Me if You Can* feel. It stirred anger into my fear. Laura was energized, her judgment questionable at best, and if I could have peered into her brain, I believed I would have seen her thoughts racing.

Laura, in flight mode. Laura, gone.

CHAPTER TWENTY

Catch Me If You Can

Hope is a horrible thing, you know....It's a plague. It's like walking around with a fishhook in your mouth and someone just keeps pulling it and pulling it.

~ Ann Patchett, *State of Wonder*

A week went by and we heard nothing. The police officer who took our report seemed weary of coming to our home. Flat affect, poor eye contact, in a hurry to be out our door. The officers had met Laura numerous times, talking with her after past retrievals. Did they realize she collected their business cards? The first time she pulled a small collection of the police cards out of her pocket, flashing the faces of the officers and commenting on their smiles or their hair or their good looks, I let out a small gasp. They reminded me of baseball cards my son had collected. Laura shrugged, smiling only slightly as she muttered, "My life."

Did this officer think she might outfox them, or was he simply bored, knowing she had no car this time to add to the excitement of the chase? No possible charges to press as when she had fled in our car?

After we had retrieved Laura from Cleveland, she had told us she had been driven there by a twenty-year-old male she and EunKyung had met at the mall near the movie theater. She had stayed with him for a week at his sister's apartment in a middle-class section of Cleveland until his sister returned from a trip. Then he had dropped her off somewhere in East Cleveland where she had slept in the park at night, cooked or babysat for strangers who would feed her, surviving until she had been spotted by the police as that "white child" being pushed from a car. I had made a futile attempt to press charges on the twenty-year-old male. I learned that I could have filed charges against him if he had taken my *car* to Cleveland without my permission, but not for transporting my sixteen-year-old daughter!

But that had been during the hot and humid days of summer, three months before Laura's Friday the Thirteenth October getaway. The calendar inched toward November. November in Ohio can be fickle, often cold and icy and snowy. How could Laura survive without cold-weather clothes and shoes? Without a car or phone?

And how would *I* survive? For I had not yet recovered from all her running. A few hours missing, missing overnight, three days missing, ten days missing, twenty-one days missing, memories of East Cleveland in the dark of night, a stripped-down and damaged car, bleeding feet... All imprinted on my brain.

The police seemed more annoyed than concerned, but maybe my expectations were too high. There had been no crime committed. No speeding vehicle. And they were not a teenage-runaway retrieval agency. I realized I would have to be the primary facilitator in getting her home. This rescue was on me.

One evening, Kevin, Pete, Ryan, and I sat in our home with about twenty of our friends, making search plans, digging through cell phone records, and mapping out sections of our city. Elizabeth was in the middle of her senior year of high school. We updated her on our progress but kept it to a minimum so she would not be derailed from her own schoolwork and college plans. Kevin had the map expertise and assigned individuals to parts of the city for them to cover. There was no Facebook at the time, so I relied on emails, sending them to everyone I knew, asking them to forward them on. I again registered Laura with the National Center for Missing and Exploited Children, something I did each time she went missing. For me, it was like calling a life-line. No one there ever said, "She's gone? *Again?*" And they rejoiced with me each time I called to say Laura was home. We duplicated the posters with Laura's photo on them sent to me by the NCMEC and walked the streets of Worthington and Columbus, handing them out to businesses and posting them on telephone poles and bulletin boards all over town. We plodded along in the Ohio State campus area from Planned Parenthood to McDonald's to bookstores to bars to restaurants that lined High Street, the main entry into the university world, sharing the posters and talking with anyone who would listen.

After a teenaged nephew of one of my friends was able to connect a name and address to a phone number from Laura's cell phone records, which the Worthington police had claimed was impossible to trace, I lost faith in the police being any help. I called and met with a private detective. Two days and a few hundred dollars later, I fired him. A timid man, well-groomed and dressed in an expensive-looking suit, he might have been exemplary at finding a cheating spouse. But he would have no idea where to find a slippery little Asian female who in the past had managed to survive on her own in a ghetto.

The fear that I would never see Laura again, the pain in my back from a bulging disc, and the burning fire in my stomach pushed me into despair. I felt so alone. So isolated. And then those frightening visions I experienced of me leaping off the balcony!

Was I experiencing suicidal thoughts?

I did not want to die! Is this what my depressed patients had meant when they had told me, "I would never take my own life, but I have these intrusive thoughts"?

I was frightened of the situation and frightened by my own mind. I needed to stay alive; I needed to find Laura. I felt safe when Kevin was home in the evenings, and I found myself keeping in touch with my friends during the day, fearful of being alone with myself.

My dear friend Susan called me one afternoon after an appointment she had with her doctor. She had relayed Laura's story to him. Dr. Murakami knew me and Laura, having treated her in the past for her depression.

"Dr. Murakami said that if it were his daughter who was missing, he'd hire a bounty hunter," Susan confidently told me.

"A bounty hunter?" I had no knowledge of what a bounty hunter actually did. Didn't that involve guns, tattoos, and major crime?

"Yes, Kathy. A bounty hunter. So," Susan went on, "I asked him how one goes about hiring a bounty hunter. He said, 'Tell her to look in the phone book and call a bail bondsman.'"

Armed with hope and trust in Dr. Murakami and with a smidgen of Susan's confidence, along with total ignorance of what I could be getting myself into, I searched the phone book for listings of bail bondsmen. I picked one in downtown Columbus and called.

"Hello," I responded when a female voice answered the phone. "I would like to know if you have any bounty hunters who work for you."

"Yes, we do," she politely replied. "We have one."

Oh, I thought with disappointment, only one? I thought there'd be a bevy from which to choose. What if he's not exactly what I need? But I had no idea what qualities would make up the perfect bounty hunter to meet my needs.

"I would like to hire him," I asserted without wavering, surprising myself. "Can you tell me how I can get in touch with him?"

Without hesitation, she gave me the name and phone number of Stewart Wackman. What a perfect name for a bounty hunter. Could he be for real?

I thanked her as I wondered how many calls like mine she received on a daily basis. Her voice was efficient and kind, making it easier for me to make one more request: Since Laura had fled with comfort to the predominantly black neighborhood of East Cleveland in the past, I added while holding my breath, "Oh, um, one more thing. Um, I need him to be black." My boldness felt empowering.

Without hesitation or surprise in her voice, she responded, "Oh, he's black. And he's big too!"

A few hours later, my sought-after bounty hunter was standing at my front door. "Nice to meet you. I'm Stewart Wackman," he said, offering his hand and a soft smile. Well over six feet tall, muscular and wide—and yes, black—he was soft-spoken in a gentle-giant kind of way.

Stewart looked over different pictures of Laura, asked questions about her personality and interests, and took cell phone numbers from the most recent weeks. I explained that she probably would not be found in suburbia but more likely in the inner city or campus areas, and I explained as much as I knew of her time spent in East Cleveland. After talking for almost two hours, I told him I really wanted him to help me.

"What do I do next?" I asked.

He explained cost, which meant nothing to me. This was my first experience at hiring a bounty hunter. Not only did I lack knowledge of how to comparison shop, I was willing to pay whatever was needed. I signed a contract and gave him several hundred dollars in cash to get started with his search. I did not know the sum would amount to thousands in the coming weeks, but it wouldn't have mattered if I had.

Stewart shook my hand again. His parting words before walking out my front door were, "We'll keep in close touch. Call you in the morning."

I collapsed against the closed door, gasping for breath.

Laughter escaped from deep in my throat as I wiped away my tears.

Shit! I had just hired a bounty hunter.

Me!

And *hope* reinserted its hook.

CHAPTER TWENTY-ONE

Drop Back Ten and Punt

All of earth's creatures have, hidden within their beings,
a wild uncontrollable urge to punt!
~ Charles M. Schulz, *The Complete Peanuts, Vol. 6:*
1961-1962

Stewart and I met every few days in the lobby of Southeast Mental Health Center in downtown Columbus. We would walk down the hall to my office and he would share his strategy with me, plot the next move, and sometimes I would hand over more money for his services. The lobby of Southeast was one of the few places in town where we would not stand out: me, a small, white female in her early fifties who more often than not received the annoying label of "sweet;" and Stewart, a burly, dark-skinned, overly large young man who could easily be mistaken for the mental health center's security guard. We were an odd couple, indeed. But an odd, fierce couple on a mission.

Laura had been missing for ten days when I hired Stewart. I had tried everything I knew of and everything I was good at to find Laura. Everything had failed. But I was not going to give up. It was time to try something else, to regroup my forces, to limit the possibility of further loss. Stewart was my *drop back ten and punt* solution.

Finding a missing teen was new for Stewart. He had worked in Brooklyn and now in Columbus, doing the usual work that bounty hunters do, capturing fugitives and criminals for a monetary reward. He scoured Laura's cell phone records, looked

through photos, and interviewed Laura's friends. He had part-
ners following up on leads, even if it meant traveling to another
city.

Laura was neither a fugitive from the law nor a criminal. But
Stewart was intrigued by her story and had empathy for me. As
he sorted through Laura's photos while sitting at my kitchen
table the first day we met, I believed he understood what was
going on with her. He asked detailed questions about the photos
I showed him, noticing changes in her expression and mood.

"Look how happy her eyes are here," he commented, "and
how sad and despondent she is in this picture." I never asked him,
but I wondered how he understood the subtle mood changes of
a person with bipolar depression. He seemed to be familiar with
the ups and downs of moods as well as the shame Laura could
be feeling about her own behavior, making it more and more
difficult for her to return home the longer she was gone. When
I shared with him that after she was found in Cleveland she had
told me she had "been through hell," he never asked me, "Then
why does she keep running away?" He understood her illness at
a level that enabled him to focus on what it would take to bring
her home. My trust in Stewart never wavered.

Will and I would talk on the phone about Laura, but he
did not actively help with the searching or the costs. That was
on me, just as her adoption had been and just as most of the
parenting of her had been. I was and would always be *her mom*.

While Stewart was searching, I grew stronger with the support
of Kevin, my friends, and the NCMEC. Laura was listed as an
"endangered runaway" on the NCMEC posters and website
because of her mental health diagnosis and being without her
medication. NCMEC was founded by John and Reve Walsh

after their son, Adam, had been abducted in 1981. His severed head was found two weeks later in a drainage canal. I remember watching the news about Adam's abduction and death, never imaging that in two shorts years my own son would die. And that seventeen years later, the aftermath of the Walshes' tragedy would support me through the experience of my own missing child.

NCMEC linked me with a volunteer support person from Team HOPE whom I could call when needed and who would call periodically to check up on me. She had lived my nightmare with her daughter. Like the Compassionate Friends after Shawn died, NCMEC and Team HOPE supported me and kept me breathing through the dark times. My volunteer, Sarah, understood my unspoken fears and irrational thoughts. No judgments made. Sarah also understood the fleeing and shame and guilt that accompanied Laura's depression, for her daughter had also been diagnosed with bipolar disorder. Sarah offered hope and compassion that no one else in my life could offer, because she not only understood what I was going through, but she also understood Laura. I will remain forever grateful for Sarah and for the life of little Adam Walsh.

Laura became a poster child for runaway prevention. She had chosen the best time of the year to run, for November is National Runaway Prevention Month. I took advantage of it. Kevin and I met with Betty Montgomery, the Attorney General of Ohio, who arranged a television interview to bring attention to the plight of runaway and missing children. Kevin appeared in the interview, along with Montgomery. His voice was calm and articulate on our local TV station's evening news, while idyllic scenes of Worthington alternating with photos of Laura were flashed on the screen. *How could anyone run away from this?* Montgomery arranged for me to be part of a four-member panel on Ohio News Network for a thirty-minute television presentation on missing children. I struggled to push the face of the previous year's *mother of a missing child* out of my mind. Her daughter, nine-year-old Erika Baker, had disappeared while walking her aunt's dog. A man later confessed and was imprisoned for her murder. Erika Baker's body has never been found.

∞

On November 16, a week before Thanksgiving, Vickie and I were driving to a photography exhibit downtown where a physician friend of mine was showing some of his work. Vickie had called to say, "You need to get out of the house." She was right, for as the days and weeks went by with no word from Laura, I was becoming despondent. When we were almost to the exhibit, my cell phone rang. It was Stewart.

"Meet me at the Giant Eagle near campus in about thirty minutes! I'll have Laura." His words stunned me. All the hours and days of waiting, and thirty-three days later, she finally might have been found. I felt sick to my stomach. My hands shook as Vickie and I sat waiting in my car in the Giant Eagle parking lot. I could feel my heart beating fast and loud in my ears. Vickie sat in the passenger seat, nervously sucking in the smoke from the one cigarette I've ever allowed anyone to smoke in my car.

Miraculously, our work had paid off. Stewart had questioned several people from the phone numbers on Laura's cell. He went back and questioned some of the people again. And again. "I knew I wasn't getting the whole truth from this one guy," he told me later. "So, I just kept goin' back, leaning on him a bit, lettin' him know he'd be in *big* trouble if anything happened to her." Stewart explained he would "throw in a little more attitude" with each visit he made to him.

After Laura's picture had appeared on television during the interview with Kevin, Stewart had received a phone call from one of the young guys he had questioned several times.

"You know that Laura girl you've been looking for?" he queried Stewart. Then he said the magic words. "*Well, I know where she is.*"

He helped Stewart lure Laura to a Tim Horton's near the Ohio State campus. Stewart drove there, walked up to Laura, and identified himself.

"Laura?"

"Yeah?" she responded, willingly revealing her identity.

"Your mom sent me. I'm here to take you home."

After securing Laura in the back seat of his car, Stewart drove to the Giant Eagle and pulled up beside my car. I didn't understand why Laura had complied so passively with Stewart. Maybe she was tired too. Maybe she was homesick and ready to let go and come home. Maybe she wanted to be with family for Thanksgiving. Or maybe it was Stewart's size and his threatening promise: "I won't put the cuffs on you if you don't give me a hard time."

"She looks good," he yelled through his rolled-down window. "I told Laura we are heading to the hospital and she can see you there." Dr. Carol had prearranged another hospital admission, effective as soon as Laura was found.

Laura, looking small and demure, sat alone in the middle of

the back seat, protective glass between her and Stewart, who sat in the driver's seat. I gave an exhausted wave to Laura.

She hesitated, then gave a faint smile and waved back.

CHAPTER TWENTY-TWO

Round-Trip Ticket, Please

All journeys have secret destinations of which the traveler is unaware.

> ~ Martin Buber, The Legend of the Baal-Shem

I sat beside Laura at OSU Harding Hospital while she was interviewed by the intake nurse. The words slipped from my mouth in a whisper as my eyes fell upon the dark red and blue ink forming Chinese letters in a yin-yang in the center of my daughter's chest.

"I sure hope that's not permanent."

Laura glanced at the nurse, then focused on me.

"Yep, it is. Got it yesterday." Her grin infused light and energy into the closet-sized psychiatric intake room.

My eyes slid from the glistening ink—*was it even dry yet?*—to Laura's dancing brown eyes. I knew. After thirty-three days of her being on the lam, concern over a yin-yang tattoo on my sixteen-year-old daughter's chest was not the mountain I would choose to die on. She was alive. She was safe. I wanted to capture the moment forever.

I reached for her hand and held it tight. Its familiar soft warmth temporarily soothed me, dimming my memory of the agony I had endured during the past several months. *Where had she been this time? What had she done?*

Laura's small hand. Still child-sized and easy to contain. So incongruent with her adventurous wanderings. We had survived standing on the edge, yet I feared there would be taller mountains to climb in the future. I was emotionally and physically exhausted. I needed to save my energy, not deplete it on a tattoo.

∞

Laura was hospitalized for a week, then transferred to a residential center for three more weeks. On Thanksgiving Day, Kevin, Pete, and I, along with Laura's friend Jordan, brought a Thanksgiving meal to Laura at the residential center. Laura was not happy. She didn't like being "locked up" or having been put there. We sat in a small room, Laura next to Jordan, who was home on break from his freshman year at Boston College. She shared most of her words and food with Jordan, throwing glances my way with her sad eyes.

I thought back to the October evening several weeks earlier when I had appeared on the ONN television presentation on missing children. One of the panel members was a staff member from Huckleberry House, an organization that had served as a crisis shelter for teens and young adults since 1970. It had evolved to include services to help prevent or intervene in the crises that compel teens to run away. I talked with two of the "Huck House" staff at the ONN studio after the show. When I told them Laura's physician had prearranged a hospitalization and a follow-up residential placement for when Laura was found, they expressed concern.

"Oh, that's not going to help her," one of them had blurted out.

"If Laura has been running and then you confine her, she'll feel panic," the other staff member tried to explain when she saw the startled look on my face. "It's going to make her want to run more."

"I have to keep her in a safe place. Just until the medication takes effect, that's all," I said, feeling unsure of myself while wanting to believe that Dr. Carol was giving the best advice. Also, I was crazed with fear that Laura might run again and never be found. I knew there was no magic pill to cure it all, but I believed the right medication could stabilize her so she would be more receptive to therapy and support.

The Huckleberry House staff had worked for years with runaway teens, but they were not mothers. They did not know the horrific feeling of trying to breathe while your child is missing. Besides, the staff members were young, appearing closer to Laura's age than to mine. So, how could they know for sure what was best for Laura? They did not understand that sometimes children leave home and never return. Sometimes they die.

~~∞~~

My heart was heavy that Thanksgiving. Although I was more than thankful that Laura was alive, safe, secure, and getting evaluated for medication, I wondered whether this was the best place for her. She was the only one there who was not in the custody of Children Services. Many of the other teens had delinquency charges and had been placed there by a juvenile court. Laura did not fit in. Will and I were offered the opportunity to place her in the custody of Children Services so the cost of treatment would be covered. But we declined. It was one thing about which Will and I readily agreed. It would certainly have saved money, but we would have lost all decision-making abilities about Laura's care.

Laura had been started on the medication Depakote while hospitalized at OSU Harding. As Dr. Carol had promised, it calmed her. Since Depakote is known to cause serious birth defects if taken during the first trimester, a pregnancy test was performed shortly after her admission to the hospital and prior to her starting the drug. A second pregnancy test was performed while she was in the residential center. She had been on Depakote about three weeks. The first test was negative. The second one was positive. The first test was performed too early in her pregnancy to show positive.

The residential center's social worker met with Laura and me to discuss the results of the positive pregnancy test. Since she had been on the medication for several weeks, the chances of a birth defect affecting the brain, heart, limbs, or cleft palate was significant. Laura did not want to be pregnant. She wanted to terminate the pregnancy. The residential center informed us they would take her off Depakote and all other medications because of the risk to the baby while she remained at the center. But if she decided to terminate the pregnancy, she would need to leave and not be allowed to return and continue treatment of any kind through the center. In short, Laura could remain at the center on no medication if she continued the pregnancy. Or she could return home, terminate the pregnancy if she chose, and continue medication under the care of Dr. Carol.

I supported Laura's choice. She was released to home a week before her seventeenth birthday. Since she was very early in her pregnancy, her physician suggested she have a medical abortion procedure, enabling her to avoid anesthesia and surgery. Dr. Carol not only continued to help her with her mental health medications but also gave her therapy and emotional support.

Laura was quiet and slept poorly during the first weeks at home. She and I spent time together going to the bookstore, or shopping, or out to lunch. Quiet time. Both of us seeming to be okay with the silent spaces between us. Laura seemed preoccupied, and I felt an immense sadness coming from her. Or maybe it was my own sadness I felt but just didn't know how to put into words.

~~∞~~

Village Academy relaxed its rules and terminated my financial contract, freeing me from six months of my nine-month commitment. Laura had brought more excitement to their school than expected, and they were probably relieved she was transferring. So, I was able to hold onto my money and they to their bucolic façade. Laura returned to Worthington's Linworth campus in January 2001 to continue her junior year of high school. She remained on Depakote, which did give more stability to Laura's mood with less irritability and depression. But two problems lingered: guilt and anxiety. Guilt over the pregnancy, the abortion, and the pain she knew she had inflicted on others, mostly me, as she would later reveal. Guilt was a direct link to her anxiety, which she was struggling to learn how to manage. Anxiety made her want to escape. To flee. To take a trip.

Laura stayed on her medication and engaged in therapy through January and February, but as the March spring winds came, Laura's anxiety ratcheted up. She hated the way Depakote made her feel tired and gain weight. Her compliance became sporadic. It seemed more of a struggle for her to contain herself within the wall of a classroom. She grew restless. Her focus was poor and her thoughts were racing.

In bipolar language, Laura had one more itch to scratch, one more trip to take. A short, unplanned trip with a big lesson for Laura and Kevin and me. This trip started mid-week in the month of March. She went to school but didn't come home and didn't respond to my phone calls. A restless seventeen-year-old high school junior who had lost contact with most of her friends after being on the lam and then being hospitalized for most of the year, Laura felt she didn't fit in with her old high school crowd anymore. A depleted mother, tired of jumping hurdles, leaping fences, and penetrating walls, I felt a void of strength and courage.

When Friday morning came with still no word from Laura, I announced to Kevin, "I'm going to Laura's Dr. Carol appointment today without Laura."

Without looking at me, Kevin nodded and announced, "I've decided to take the day off and go visit my mother. Should be back by dinner."

Kevin had never visited his mother without me since we'd been married, and rarely at all since she had been moved to a dementia-care facility in Toledo. He hated the three-hour drive, she probably wouldn't recognize him, and being around her made him anxious. Although I was surprised by Kevin's decision to make the trip, we didn't discuss it further.

I felt hopeful later that afternoon as I drove home from meeting with Dr. Carol, a wise and kind woman who seemed to be fond of Laura, and who, more importantly, understood Laura and the forces colliding within her. That Friday, Dr. Carol focused on me. On my pain. She sensed the gnawing worry and anxiety that clung so relentlessly to me.

"Laura is a resilient survivor, Kathy. She's amazingly resourceful. You are suffering. It's time to let go."

I couldn't believe what she was telling me, and my shock at her words must have been noticeable for she smiled softly and continued to explain. "The way to help Laura now is to trust her. Let go a bit. If she doesn't want to stay in school, she can quit and take her GED."

"Quit school? In her junior year?" I asked.

"She's very bright and she will figure it out. Laura knows you are there for her," Dr. Carol added. Then we discussed how Laura could proceed with disenrolling from the Worthington School District, obtaining her GED, and continuing with classes at the community college.

It was after 6:30 by the time I pulled into my driveway. I was eager to share Dr. Carol's advice and parting words with Kevin. "Go home, focus on you. Take care of yourself and your marriage."

But Kevin's car wasn't in the garage. "Should be back by dinner," he had said that morning.

My feelings went from hopeful to worried, then frantic to despairing as dinner hour came and went and late evening approached. No response to my phone calls to Kevin. No Laura. Not a word from either one. I cried myself to sleep, waking Saturday morning with swollen eyes, an emptiness in the pit of my stomach, and a deep sense of abandonment.

Saturday I was consoled by a friend as I unloaded on her, but there was not a soul on earth who could really understand what I was feeling. I continued to call Kevin and Laura and several of Laura's friends, finally receiving enough of a message from Kevin that told me he had never intended to visit his mother. Where he was, I had no clue, only that he took a trip.

Late Sunday afternoon, Laura called. She had received word from a friend that I was alone and that Kevin was gone. "Mom, I'm sorry. You need me to come home?"

"Yes, I need you to come home."

Laura and I didn't talk much. I did tell her what Dr. Carol had said about getting her GED and Laura wanted to "think about it."

Sunday evening, close to midnight, Kevin came home. "Hi, Hon," he said after finding me calming my agitation with a hot bath. Kevin looked and spoke as if he had never been among the missing. I was mute.

He walked out of the bathroom and came upon Laura with her fists clenched and eyes ablaze, words of chastisement spewing from her mouth. Somewhere in the midst of, "How could you do this?" and "Don't you care how upset you made Mom?" Kevin interrupted her with, "Now you know how it feels."

∞

A close friend and surrogate aunt to Laura sent me a greeting card after Laura had been retrieved by my bounty hunter. The picture on the front shows a woman sitting on a sunny beach. She is smiling. Inside is written:

"A trip is what you take whenever you are tired of whatever it is you've been taking."

What had Laura been tired of taking when she fled our home? And Kevin too? Tired of what *he* had been taking?

The card was my friend's way of giving me support and comfort. Of offering another point of view. Of trying to shed some understanding on Laura's fleeing and running and high-risk meandering. To transform them into a simple four-letter word. *Trip…*

…what you take whenever you are tired of whatever it is you've been taking.

CHAPTER TWENTY-THREE

Traveling Together

"Yes, Piglet?"

"Nothing," said Piglet, taking Pooh's paw. "I just wanted to be sure of you."

~ A.A. Milne, *The House at Pooh Corner*

We had all reached our tipping point that weekend in March, and I was on the edge of my own mammoth "Aha!" moment. I knew Laura's response to crisis was to take flight, but as I focused more on my own response to crisis, I realized that mine was to fight. And, my fight and Laura's flight were colliding. When Laura took flight, I pursued. When I pursued, Laura felt trapped and wanted to escape—to take flight.

"It doesn't mean she is running from you. She's probably running from herself. From a situation that she doesn't want to face or she doesn't know how to deal with. You might have to give her the space she needs before she settles down."

I started to value the advice the Huckleberry House staff had given me. I knew Laura wasn't running from me. I had always known that Laura wasn't running from me or because of me. I just didn't know how to soothe her, to calm her, or to teach her how to soothe herself.

Laura would say she never had any "true mania," but she admits to periods of heightened energy, racing thoughts, and creativity. I have heard her pressured speech during those times and have watched her excessively and obsessively fill notebooks full of her writings, a behavior called hypergraphia. During the years of her running, I had realized that as painful as it was for me, her need to escape had to do with the anxiety that comes with having bipolar depression. I also knew that any time there was a real or perceived crisis, or if Laura felt she had failed, she would respond by fleeing. As a mother, I wanted to help her find the sweet spot of balance between hyperenergetic highs and immobilizing lows—the equilibrium point where life is good.

Considering the extraordinary events in Laura's life—her adoption history, her reconnection with her birth family, her diagnosis of a mood disorder—it was easy to understand Laura's need to run. To flee. To take flight.

∞

I needed to lean on Dr. Carol's wisdom. *The way to help Laura now is to trust her. It's time to let go a bit.* Yes, of course. Part of the job of parenting is letting go and giving our children wings. Isn't that what we are supposed to do? I think of the Chinese finger trap, often considered to be a mere toy. Even as a child, when I placed a finger into each end and pulled, I understood the lesson to be learned: When I stopped pulling, I was free. I could breathe, relax, accept that there are some things over which we are powerless. Letting go gives us freedom.

Letting go was difficult for me. For me, letting go takes courage.

Considering the impact of the extraordinary events on my own life—Shawn's unexpected death, my divorce, even my father's sudden death when I was in college—it is easy to comprehend my fear of loss. My need to hold on. To fight.

∞

In the midst of all this, Kevin was, like Laura, more inclined to flee than to fight. Oh, Kevin had done his share of fighting—navigating searches throughout Central Ohio, rescuing Laura from strange places, conveying our despair to television news media, even remaining silent about all the money I had spent on search and rescue. Kevin admired my tenacity, but when it reached the level of an angry pit bull, he retreated. My tenacity was pushing him away. Fortunately, it was a rare event to push him away physically, but I was doing it emotionally. His weekend away made me realize Kevin and I had some major repair work to do on our relationship.

While juggling Laura's safety and my relationship with Kevin, my own physical and mental health had deteriorated. I grieved the loss of the hours that Laura and I used to fill with talks, laughter, shopping, or transporting her and her friends to the skating rink. I wanted to once again have the predictable closeness Kevin and I had shared during the first years of our marriage. More than anything, I missed *me*, the one who had been filled with energy and resilience. I missed the *me* that was not afraid to do new things and let my children soar. The one who had fought her way back after Shawn had died and after divorce and through years as a single parent. But in my panic and desperate attempts to fix things, to keep everyone safe, to hold on and make permanent even the impermanent, I was creating my own isolation. And I was losing myself.

<hr>

Our family had reached a crisis, a tipping point. This tipping point offered each of us the opportunity to look at our situation through the eyes of the others. It was an opportunity for change.

Laura and I talked about her dropping out of school and what that would mean to her. On Monday after her return home, I accompanied her to the administration office of Worthington schools and she withdrew. I took her downtown to the Ohio Department of Education office and she applied to sit for her GED. On Friday, I dropped her off in the morning for her test.

"You can pick me up. I'm done," she informed me when she called at noon. After she had received her scores in the mail a week later, she carried her GED certificate to Columbus State Community College and enrolled in her first college classes. She was no longer a high school junior, but a college student.

I thought it might be difficult for me to let go of seeing her reach the traditional milestones of senior prom, high school graduation, college selection, and moving into a college dorm miles from home, but it was not. The relief I felt from having a reprieve from all the drama of the past few years was immense.

On the weekend of her eighteenth birthday, Laura moved into her own apartment located less than a mile from our home. Close enough to be sure of each other. Laura needed her own space, and being alone energized her—in a good way. I was proud of Laura and her ability to take control of her life. She did it her way. Two and a half years after sitting for her GED, she earned her associate of business degree. Eighteen months after that, she graduated with a bachelor's in business and marketing.

Laura having her own space gave Kevin and me room to focus on each other again. Kevin had a job change and I returned to the Ohio State University Medical Center as a nurse practitioner on an inpatient psychiatric unit. Kevin and I started *dating* again, committing hours each day to each other, relearning what drew us together when we first met. We made a commitment and stuck to it, each of us pushing the other when it was needed. It took more than a year, but we finally took a long-overdue trip to the beach together, alone.

∞

Another change for Laura and me that took place after our family's "tipping point" weekend was a mutual commitment to communicate and stay connected. I put ICE (in case of emergency) next to her name in my phone, and Laura programmed my number into her phone under *ICE-MOM*. That way, either of us would be reached if there were an emergency. For this to work smoothly, I had to be watchful not to worry and she needed to be vigilant to have faith in herself. This was challenging for both of us, for Laura and I were like wounded warriors with PTSD.

With time, Laura learned to turn more to her family for support, avoiding the need to flee. Most often she would turn to me. A sense of urgency, an immediate need, an event that had a time-critical response would occur, and I would respond. I would always be there. I became conditioned to respond to any real or perceived crisis. Helping Laura, knowing she had survived and that she was still in my life, was food to my soul. I needed to find my own sweet spot—the equilibrium point where life is good. My job was to learn how to keep my life balanced, to be there for Laura without becoming Pavlov's dog reacting to the crisis bell. Finding *my* sweet spot, I grew to realize, would probably take a lifetime.

PART THREE

~

As Korea is waiting for the earth to spin,
for streaks of light to brighten its eastern sky,
in that quiet moment there is a calmness
that makes Korea the most beautiful country
in the world.

~ Tucker Elliot, *The Day Before 9/11*

Laura Kathleen, once known as SeonKyung, is returning to her homeland. You believe it is mostly a wise thing to do. You want her to experience her birthland and explore her beginnings.

But you have never sent a child of yours so far away.

Of course, you are not actually doing the sending. Laura is, after all, a young adult. You know she can care for herself. After a few years of medication trials and errors, Laura finds medication that keeps her moods stable without depleting her energy. She eats well, makes exercise a priority, and works at keeping good sleep habits. As she approaches her twenty-fifth birthday, she signs a contract with Chung Dahm Learning.

Laura will teach English to Korean elementary students in Seoul. She will live just a few miles from her birth family. And far away from you. Laura living in Korea means you have to mother from a distance.

Unlike the impulsive, running-away trips of her adolescence, Laura's trip to Korea is an anticipated departure. You are no longer the frantic, fear-driven searcher for your daughter but the support and encouragement giver, the behind-the-scenes manager, and the you-go-girl cheerleader. For this getaway, you are Laura's accomplice.

You watch and help Laura plan her trip to Korea. You reflect on the morning Shawn left for his first Boy Scout camp-out. As you help him pack and send him off with a gentle push of enthusiasm, you believe you are helping his wings to grow. You are not the least bit concerned about his safety. In fact, the morning starts with fun and excited expectations, not fears. For Shawn, it is a paradise. Wildlife, cliffs, and waterfalls cascading into deep cool gorges. Yet, your son dies. He falls from a cliff in paradise. You are not there to pull him back and keep him safe here on your side of the world. He never returns.

Deep within, you carry a shadow of guilt about Shawn's accident. Not logical, probably. But how much are you to blame? Should you have taught him to be a timid, cautious child? Instead, you nurtured and encouraged his enthusiasm, the way he embraced life. Oh, how you loved that about him! Does that make you an accomplice in creating his adventurous spirit?

As you watch Laura plan her trip to her birthland—walking on the edge of her beginnings, peering over—you want to protect her. You want to grab her and infuse her with common sense. You want to clip her free-spirited wings—just a little bit.

Oh, please be careful, Laura. Don't get too close to the edge.

CHAPTER TWENTY-FOUR

In the Land of the Morning Calm

I found that the more I lived abroad, the more American I discovered I was.

~ Daniel J. Boorstin

"These Koreans are driving me crazy!"

Six words and three seconds after answering my phone in Ohio, I knew the honeymoon in Korea was over.

"Honey, you're one of them," I told my daughter with a lightness in my voice. I wasn't sure whether Laura needed to hear words of comfort or humor, but I couldn't help chuckling to myself.

"No, Mom. I'm an American."

I listened as Laura vented to me from the other side of the world. "There are these annoying fruit trucks that roam the streets at all hours with loud speakers...and, why can't they chew with their mouths closed?...I can't stand to hear them eat. And they all do it! Oh, another thing...I'm NOT taking the subway anymore! I'll be taking a taxi. These people push. Do you realize what that's like? And me being so short. Makes it worse. It's impossible for me to walk around here without being pushed by these Koreans. It's so rude. I just think it's rude...you know how I need my space!"

I was Laura's mother. With patience, I had learned to let her vent. Through practice, I had learned to give short responses, such as "Oh my" or "Wow" or "How are you feeling now?"

"So, you suggest I avoid the subways when I'm there?" I asked when there was a pause in Laura's venting, urging the conversation to shift toward discussion of my trip to Korea in June. Kevin and I had signed up as participants in *Tour Korea! 2009,* a tour offered to adoptive families by CHSFS. "Only twelve more weeks and you can guide me around Seoul," I told Laura cheerfully.

"It's that long?" she asked. "I can't wait until you're here." She hastily added, "I'll be fine, Mom. You know me, I'm just having one of my *moments*. I'm fine." She wanted to soothe me, not be a stimulus for my worrying, which she knew I could do quite well.

After our conversation ended, I sat at my dining room table with my tea and peanut butter toast, watching snow slowly drift from the morning sky and come to rest on the tall white pines outside my window. I pictured Laura moving around her tiny, windowless apartment on the other side of the world.

It was nighttime in Seoul. While I finished breakfast, perhaps Laura would be preparing a snack; while I drove to work, perhaps she'd be watching a movie; and while I prepared for my day at the office, perhaps she'd be posting on her blog. According to the orientation materials sent to Laura when she signed her teaching contract, she was right on schedule with her adjustment to living in a different culture. The agency had described a honeymoon period, followed by annoyance and some anger—maybe even depression—before she could expect, *hopefully,* to adjust to life in South Korea. Laura was following the path as predicted, even though she was "one of them."

I was surprised she even had a honeymoon period, for her anxiety and doubts about spending a year in her land of birth had peaked the week before she left. And I was worried, too. As I'd helped her prepare for the trip, I had moments when I felt Laura might as well be planning a trip to the moon. South Korea seemed so far away, so foreign, and so unknown. What dangers could befall my adventurous daughter? Would her adolescent risk-taking behaviors—painful memories I had never been able to fully extinguish—resurface in a foreign country? What if she loved it in Korea so much she would want to stay?

But during the first three weeks in Seoul, she posted pictures on her blog—of karaoke with her fellow teachers, of shoes she planned to purchase while there, her hookah bar visit, Korean food, and more shoes. She shared stories about her students and spoke warmly about her classroom and teaching. I enjoyed her honeymoon, albeit brief. While she navigated through her days, I slept better, and as she unwound late at night, my mornings had been more relaxing.

∞

I noticed the snow falling faster, covering our lawn with a clean blanket of white fluff. I placed my shoes in a bag, pulled on my boots, and slipped on my winter coat. I could almost hear the echoing cacophony of screaming fruit trucks winding their way through the narrow streets of Seoul. As I backed my car out of the driveway, I turned up the music, attempting to smother the annoying open-mouth chewing of "those Koreans." Later, as I sat at my desk at work, I felt the suffocating closeness of my daughter's culture pushing against me, making it hard to breathe.

Lost

The call came in the middle of the night—her night—forty days into Laura's stay in Korea.

"Mom? I'm lost," Laura said from the other side of the world. Words timid, tight, and barely audible. I thought I heard sniffles. Then silence.

I was at work, and an all-too-familiar wave of fear and panic rolled through my gut, crashing up into my chest. I wanted to protect Laura.

"I know he did this on purpose. He knew he was leaving me off at the wrong place." Laura's words spilled out as I stood, then paced along the dark hallway outside my office, cell phone to my ear. *Breathe in, breathe out,* I told myself.

Her call pierced my afternoon. It was 2 p.m., making it 3 a.m. Seoul time. Deliberate deep breathing helped to slow my racing heart and clear my head. Clear enough that I could assess the situation fairly well, even with me at work in Columbus,

Ohio, and Laura at some unknown location in, *I hoped*, Seoul, South Korea.

Laura's words were thick. I imagined them moving sluggishly through her brain. After a night of singing, dancing, drinking, or whatever young adult expats would be doing at a Korean *noraebang,* she had taken a cab back to her apartment. I imagined that as she watched the cab driver pull away, Laura looked around and realized she had no idea where she was.

My twenty-five-year-old daughter was standing in the country where she was born. Yet she was lost.

I suspected she had been drinking, but she was not drunk. If she had been drunk, I would probably have heard her anger and the use of the f-word to curse about the cab driver. When sober, she did not use the f-word around me. Never. This gave me an elevated feeling of being respected, and in situations like this, it gave me leverage on evaluating her degree of sobriety. Laura was sober enough to know she was lost.

And we both realized that, even from the other side of the world, I was still her 911.

I wondered if she had me programmed into her new Korean phone as *ICE-MOM,* just as she had in her American phone. I thought back to some of the calls I'd received when Laura was younger.

...from a nightclub bathroom in Niagara Falls, Canada, to ICE-MOM in Ohio: "Mom?" followed by sniffles and sobs from my nineteen-year-old college student, "I can't find anybody I came with and I don't know how to get back to the hotel. I have no money!" *Friends found. Crisis averted.*

...from the side of the interstate, downtown Columbus: sirens, followed by her twenty-year-old voice, a quiver vibrating through her words as she fought for composure. "Mom? I'm okay. I'm going to let you talk to the police." Laura had collided with a school bus, the bus merging onto the freeway while she was merging onto the exit ramp. *Car totaled. No one hurt. Not Laura, not one child on the school bus injured.*

⚭

"Mom? I'm lost," she now said from the other side of the world.

I had never been where Laura now stood on a sidewalk in Seoul. How dark were the streets? How close was danger lurking? It would be a few more weeks before Kevin and I would travel to Korea. Laura would be there at the airport in Seoul to meet me and show me her first home, just as I had been at the airport in Chicago, twenty-four years earlier, to bring her to her forever home in America.

I wished I had clipped her free-spirited wings! Hadn't I told her to *"Please be careful"*? But she was talking, I told myself. Breathing. Crying. *She's okay. She's safe.* She might be lost, but she's *alive!* We would figure it out together, even from opposite sides of the world.

Yet I realized, *I could not be her only 911.*

"Mom? I'm lost."

"Laura, can you call EunKyung? She can help you figure out where you are. Call your sister and then call me back. Okay?"

"Oh. Okay. Didn't think of that."

A few minutes went by before my phone rang again. "Mom, EunKyung is coming to get me." Then Laura laughed. "I'm just a few blocks from the family restaurant. Can you believe that?"

Crisis averted. Suddenly Laura didn't seem so far away.

Then a call from EunKyung to me. "Don't worry, Kattee. I take care Laura. Don't worry. I take care." Her voice was soothing, almost maternal. "Love you, Kattee."

I could let go. Breathe. EunKyung was Laura's away-from-home 911.

A few days later, another phone call from EunKyung. I heard laughter in the background as she spoke, Laura standing at her side. They were at their family-owned restaurant, Jangsu Jokbal Restaurant, located in a university district in Seoul. It was famous for a four-dollar meal of a tasty and supersized fried pork patty smothered in an outstanding barbeque sauce and served with all the traditional Korean side dishes. It was economical and wildly popular with students.

EunKyung gave the phone to Laura. "I'm helping serve at the restaurant today. EunKyung must be impressed with me. She keeps patting me on the back." Laura giggled and made no mention of the frustrations she had experienced getting lost or of any more Koreans driving her crazy. "I like it when my birth family is having fun, but it's kinda hard to watch EunKyung with her mother."

"Why's that?"

"Their closeness is like us, Mom. Seeing them together makes me miss you." Before she gave the phone back to EunKyung, she added, "Love you, Mom."

Laura's mood was upbeat. It was reassuring to hear her laugh, even with her slight melancholy about missing me. Although a decade had passed since Laura's meet-up with Dr. Bergren, who had arranged her first hospital stay, it still unsettled me to hear her mood go up and down, even the gentle swings, especially when she was so far away. Mothering from a distance is difficult.

CHAPTER TWENTY-SIX

Connecting Flights

....

Life is not about how fast you run or how high you climb but how well you bounce.

~ Tigger, in *The House at Pooh Corner*

....

I dragged my wheeled carry-on luggage with my left hand, clutching my husband's hand with my right. Together we navigated the Incheon International Airport, thirty miles west of Seoul, pressed forward by a swarm of humanity, while the harsh consonants and elongated trailing vowels of the Korean language buzzed around our heads.

Arriving at Customs, I handed my passport to a solemn-faced woman. While I was questioned as to the nature of my visit, where I would stay, and how long I would be staying, I noted her downcast eyes and recalled reading that Koreans find it impolite to gaze directly at a person when addressing them, at least for more than a few seconds. Laura had given me travel warnings.

"You can't gawk at people in Korea, Mom. And you know how you love to stare," she had added with a roll of her snappy, dark eyes. Keeping Laura's words in mind, I measured out the seconds of my eye contact as I answered, trying to ignore the irrational fear that I would be denied entry into the country that now holds my daughter. As the woman raised her stamp, readying it to make its mark of acceptance on my passport, I focused my eyes downward at my waiting hands, fearing a Seinfeld moment, a Soup-Nazi-like response of "No stamp for *you!*"

She stamped my passport and returned it to me. As she lowered her head in the habitual and deeply ingrained Korean custom of bowing, I realized I had just experienced my first authentic bow. I had arrived. I felt a sudden sense of awe and gratitude that our feet were on solid—albeit foreign—ground. It felt more secure and familiar than when we were over the dark, open-mouthed waters of the Pacific Ocean after leaving San Francisco or above the frozen mountains of Russia as we approached South Korea.

The glass doors at the airport terminal slid apart. I saw her, with flowers in her hands, running toward me. Laura was trailed by her birth parents and siblings. As Laura and I, then Laura and Kevin, hugged and kissed, there were giggles from the women and verbal exchanges of "annyeong haseyo" and "hello" from Kevin and Myeong-Suk, Laura's birth father. I was beyond thrilled to see Laura and eager for all we would see and do during our visit, but I was also so sleep-deprived from the long trip that I stumbled over my words. My attempts to say "hello" and "nice to meet you" in Korean were met with laughter from everyone. More than ten years had passed since Laura's birth mother and EunKyung had visited us in Ohio, but we had never met her birth father or younger sister, EunSeon. Myeong-Suk was short and stocky with a broad face, looking much like the pictures we had viewed over the years. But unlike his photos, which gave the impression he was rigid and serious, he was animated and jovial with a smile that stretched ear to ear. EunSeon smiled shyly. She resembled her mother and was lankier and several inches taller than EunKyung and a full head taller than Laura.

Our first taxi ride in Korea took Laura, Kevin, and me and all of our luggage to the W Seoul-Walkerhill hotel, where Kevin and

I stayed for the first five days of our visit. The W will most likely remain forever at the top of my list of favorite places I have slept. It is everything its website claimed it to be: "Resting cloudlike on the slope of Mount Acha overlooking the Han river, W Seoul is only fifteen minutes from the bustling Gangnam financial and business district, yet a world away on one-hundred-eighty acres of parkland." Walking into the W made me feel important and special. We were greeted with a bow by the doorman and by every hotel staff person we encountered as we made our way to our room. We received the "big bow" that is reserved for important people. In Korea, the lower the bow, the more respect it shows. When two people meet, the older person is always shown more respect. Kevin's white head of hair was probably what earned us the "big bow."

EunKyung picked us up in her Hyundai less than twenty minutes after we had arrived at the W. She was the only member of Laura's birth family who drove a car, and she did so competently and confidently, maneuvering fearlessly through the heavy traffic. As the four of us chatted, I avoided watching the bumper-car activity outside the car window. We quickly arrived at a part of the city with narrow brick and cobblestone streets, lined with cafés, shops, and restaurants wedged tightly together. EunKyung parked her car in a tight space I would not have recognized as a parking spot, several blocks from the restaurant, requiring a long walk on uneven streets crowded with evening dinner seekers.

At some point between my walk and halfway through our meal, I became acutely aware of my exhaustion. We were being hosted by Laura's birth family at a lovely Korean barbecue-style restaurant. Yet I had trouble not focusing on my swollen feet, which felt like they had doubled in size during the twenty-four hours since I had left home.

There were seven of us—Laura, birth mother and father, EunKyung, EunSeon, Kevin, and me—sitting around the table with a built-in gas grill. In typical Korean style, beef, pork, and chicken were placed on the table for us to grill to our liking. EunSeon seemed to get the most pleasure out of doing the grilling and explaining and urging us to try the many *banchan* (side dishes, mostly spicy) that are served with Korean meals. Sticky rice was served with everything Korean, and since I loved rice, I found it easy to try almost everything by mixing a little bit of something spicy with lots of sticky rice. When EunSeon smiled and said to me, "Oh, no, Kattee, no spicy," I added an extra amount of sticky rice. My GI tract was starting to feel the impact of jet lag and appreciated my efforts.

Two strong Korean traditions were honored at dinner our first evening: gift-giving to your hosts and drinking. We were prepared for both. I had completed the gift shopping and packing while Kevin had researched Korean drinking culture. Rules for imbibing in Korea were rigid, and you could score big points with your hosts if you understood and honored them. Kevin wanted to please, so he followed the rules as he and Myeong-Suk enjoyed their *soju*. Kevin poured Myeong-Suk's drink for him, watching that his cup did not go empty. He never poured his own drink. Kevin held his cup with both hands when Myeong-Suk poured a drink for him. Using both hands is the polite gesture for accepting anything given to you in Korea. The sound of Myeong-Suk's deep chuckle and the sight of his perpetual, wide-faced smile as he and Kevin shared their *soju*, Korean style, outshined our giving of gifts that evening.

The next morning, we awakened to the view of the Han River meandering in the distance and a phone call from Laura. "The birth family wants you to come to their restaurant today." They had closed the restaurant for the day, declaring it a holiday. They would cook for us, then take us shopping for gifts.

Laura and EunKyung picked us up, both animated and talking excitedly as we made the fifteen-minute drive from the W to the family restaurant.

Birth Mother greeted us at the door, smiling and bowing as she led us to a long table located close to the kitchen. Birth Father waved to us from the kitchen where he was busy cooking, moving the frying pans around, flames visible and lapping at their black sides.

I watched them working in tandem, Myeong-Suk cooking and Hyeja bringing in the dishes, until the entire length of the table was covered with a variety of foods. They laughed and joked with each other, encouraging us to eat up, to try new foods.

Myeong-Suk and Hyeja seemed so happy. We had been told by Aun, when EunKyung and Hyeja visited the U.S., that Hyeja was so sad after giving Laura up that Myeong-Suk thought it would help her to have another baby. Over the years, Myeong-Suk covered his own sadness with alcohol. When he learned Laura was alive and doing well, he worked at drinking less and tried to learn English, in case he would someday get to see Laura again. Was it Laura's presence in Seoul that brought out the laughter and the effervescent smiles of happiness?

Losing their child had been painful, yet they had stayed together. They had remained a family. Did the thought of divorcing or separating ever occur to either of them? Or does the Korean culture forbid such thoughts?

After eating, Laura, Kevin, EunKyung, Hyeja, Myeong-Suk, EunSeon, and I headed off to Namdaemun to shop at the biggest traditional market in Korea, located in the center of Seoul. I was nudged into a small jade shop.

"Oh, Mom, look at this ring. Purple jade." Laura pulled me toward the smiling shop owner.

"You like try?" the owner asked.

I nodded in the affirmative, after Laura first answered for me. Gazing at the smooth, oval, light purple gem, I understood why it drew Laura's attention. The color pulled my thoughts back to my purple Mazda MX-3, that sweet ride Laura had enjoyed as a teen. The thin, gold rim that held the purple jade secure was like a glint from the sun, dancing on the chrome of the car's window on a bright summer day.

Then, Hyeja at my elbow and EunKyung at her side, they urged me to try the matching jade necklace. It was a beautiful deep purple, embossed on one side with a gold crane. "Keep you happy with long life, Kattee," EunKyung told me. Hyeja nodded with a big smile.

Suddenly I felt closed in. Hyeja pressing in on me, smiling, nodding, touching my arm. EunKyung's head against mine, peering at the gems, the jade.

"She say thank you," EunKyung told me. Hyeja wanted to thank me by giving me this gift. "For taking such good care of Laura, Kattee," EunKyung added. Hyeja wanted to give back to me. I accepted the beautiful necklace with the gold crane. I placed the purple jade ring on my finger and smiled, looking at my hand. My ring of purple, a color made by blending the calming stability of blue with the fierce energy of red, now rested on my finger. I looked at Hyeja, EunKyung, and Laura, all hovering around me. I could feel the fierce energy of the past that had drawn us all together—the risks, the dreams, the loss, the love. How extraordinarily odd the moment felt. How extraordinarily calm I felt.

I bowed. "Kam-sahm-ni-da," I said, thanking Hyeja. "Kam-sahm-ni-da."

It was all I could say. I knew no words in any language that could show how grateful I was for the gift of Laura.

There were no words.

CHAPTER TWENTY-SEVEN

Seoul Train

The best part about being in Seoul was exploring it with Laura, just the two of us, together.

I had needed help in finding my way in the Daegu train station, so one of the *Tour Korea! 2009* guides had herded me onto the right train car to assure I would be headed where I wanted to go, which was back to Seoul. While Kevin and the rest of the tour group would visit the southern Korean beaches and have tea with monks at a Buddhist temple, I would be spending the weekend with Laura.

"Listen for the Seoul City station announcement. They will say it clearly in Korean and repeat it again in English," had been my thoughtful instructions.

I was surprised at how calm I felt, riding by myself, passing the South Korean countryside at a speed exceeding 250 miles per hour. As I traveled on Korea's bullet train, the KTX, from Daegu to Seoul, everyone around me was a stranger. The sights and sounds unfamiliar, except for the music coming over the speaker system.

The slow, somewhat sad, plucked-string version of The Beatles' "Let It Be" soothed me. The music was so familiar, its lyrics, its words of wisdom, filled my thoughts.

I was the first to enter my train car. I settled in and watched as more passengers boarded. A young mother and her baby sat in the seats across the aisle. I felt a sense of kinship with the young woman as I watched her lovingly tend to her little girl. The mother had her dressed in a pink outfit that accentuated her beautiful black hair. Pink, like the "pink cotton clothes" Laura had been wearing when she was left at the adoption agency. The little girl appeared to be about fourteen months old, the same age as Laura when I first held her.

My thoughts turned to the young mothers at the maternity home our group had visited earlier in the day. They numbered around twenty-five young women, with most of their pregnancies nearing term. The mothers were in the process of placing their soon-to-be-born children up for adoption. Most of the mothers had no family support. In order to avoid the shame that goes with being unwed and pregnant, they would live at the maternity home until their babies were born. It was their secret. Some had told their families that they had obtained a job in another city and they planned to contrive another face-saving story when it was time to return home after giving birth. One woman told of a boyfriend she had left because he did not want a child and she refused to end the pregnancy.

It had been an emotional day for me. Probably also for the expectant mothers and for the other members in our tour group. We had talked casually—expectant mothers, the young teen adoptees in our group, and the adoptive parents—asking questions of each other and sharing openly. We, the broken-hearted people in the world, seemed to agree.

"Adoption is birth from the heart," explained a young expectant mother who planned to place her child for international adoption. In spite of the push for domestic adoptions by the Korean government, most of the women expressed a preference for international adoption. "Adopted children are more accepted and valued in countries like the United States," one woman explained, while the other expectant mothers around her nodded in agreement. Many Koreans still see bloodline as determining the qualification for family, and these expectant mothers had concern that if their babies were to be adopted within their own country, others would shun them and the child's life would be more difficult. They wanted their child to be accepted and loved.

"I want to thank you," a young Korean-American teenaged boy in our tour group had told the mothers. "Thank you for being brave enough to give up your babies." He considered himself "lucky" to have his American family, to have his answer. *Let it be.*

The music was interrupted by the sound of the loudspeaker. A voice, first in Korean, then in English, announced that we were approaching the Seoul City Station.

Looking across the aisle, I saw that the baby in pink, snuggled on her mother's back, had fallen asleep. With the baby's face turned away from me, I saw her thick black head of hair spilling onto her mother's neck. I thought of Laura when she was little. I felt content knowing she was waiting for me, full of plans for the next three days of our mother-daughter time.

∞

I made my way out of the Seoul City Station and hailed a cab. No soothing "Let It Be," just the short sounds of the Korean language as the cab driver communicated over his radio. I said hello to the driver in Korean and used English to tell him the name of my hotel, then handed him my map, pointing to where my hotel was located. I was a bit nervous, for my taxi experiences in Korea had been mixed. When Laura, who is obviously Korean and speaks some basic Korean, was with Kevin or me in a taxi, she communicated directly with the driver and we got where we needed to go without problems. But Kevin and I, traveling without her, had had the experience of being dropped off by a cab driver far from our destination a few days earlier, realizing that, in spite of our detailed map, we had been intentionally led astray. I didn't think he had misunderstood. I believed it was because we were Americans, or at least, non-Koreans. Korean cab drivers were the same as any other country's cab drivers. Most were nice; some were not.

The driver who took me to my hotel was nice, even handing me a phone to speak with someone who translated my English back into Korean for the driver, who was having trouble locating my hotel.

When he dropped me off, I panicked as I searched in the 10 p.m. darkness for the hotel's entrance. I was tempted to call Laura but thought about how silly I would sound.

"Laura, I'm lost!"

"Laura, I'm at my hotel but can't find the door! I've been left at a hotel with no door. I think I'm lost!"

Besides, she was still teaching her class, so I would have to leave a message. I walked around the building and took a turn into a short and dark alleyway where I spotted a plain metal door into the hotel, a hotel I had selected for its low cost and convenient location. I checked in and took the elevator to my small, dark room.

Not long after, Laura called.

"My Friday class is done. I'm comin' over."

She had the address and I explained how to find the elusive front door. She hung up before I could tell her to meet me in the lobby. I didn't want her to see my room.

"Mom, you can't stay here!" Laura announced, wide-eyed, when she entered my hotel room. She stared at the stained carpet and the yellowed wallpaper. She sniffed into the air.

"No way. My mother is not staying here! It's stuffy, dirty, and it stinks!" Then she spotted the exposed outlet on the wall and the coin-operated movie box. "Oh my God, Mom. No way!"

I laughed at her exasperation. I convinced her it was too late to find another place that night, I would survive one night, and I'd figure out something different for Saturday and Sunday nights.

We had a late dinner. As she was leaving to go back to her tiny apartment, she announced, "I will take care of finding the hotel for the next two nights. It's *my* job."

In the morning, we dined at an American restaurant, a favorite of Koreans as well as expats from the U.S. Then we shopped. Mostly for shoes. Before coming to Korea, I did not realize Seoul is considered to be a shopper's paradise. There was the shoe market in Dongdaemun, known for its enormous volume of shoes and low prices. But Laura wanted quality and style, so we shopped in Myeongdong. Myeongdong was one of the busiest shopping areas, filled with department stores, shopping malls, street stalls, and other shops. I went for comfort and selected a black-and-red, eye-catching, Korean-made sandal by K-Swiss. Laura picked out a new pair of Reeboks, also Korean-made, a gray-and-pink dress pump, whose picture she had posted on her blog weeks before, and a pair of sassy three-inch heels with a zipper up the back.

"I'm exhausted," I told her.

"Now aren't you glad you aren't going back to that creepy place to sleep?"

Indeed, I was. "Yes, but where *am* I sleeping?"

"Mom, you and I are going back to the W Seoul-Walkerhill," she beamed. "Because you, Kathleen, and I, Laura, deserve the very best mother-daughter weekend in Seoul!"

CHAPTER TWENTY-EIGHT

Same-Same

....

*It grieved me that I had to let you go. Above all else,
please forgive me.*
*~ I Wish for You a Beautiful Life: Letters from Korean
Birth Mothers to Their Children*

....

I sat in a café in Seoul, sipping tea.

Jane Lee, our assigned staff from *Tour Korea! 2009,* had
arranged for Kevin and Laura and me to meet with Laura's birth
family to ask and answer questions. Jane was our translator and
our tour guide of sentiments, helping us navigate the terrain of
two languages, two cultures, and an infinite range of emotions.

The café had a western feel. The booth we sat in was large,
giving us space so we didn't feel closed in. It faced a long wall
painted with a replica of Vincent van Gogh's "The Starry Night."
We sat beneath the swirling patterns that rolled like waves across
one entire wall of the café, the radiant white and yellow lights
of the painted crescent moon, the stars shining through the dark
blues of the sky. Laura had been drawn to van Gogh in grade
school, one year adding "a book about van Gogh's paintings" to
her Christmas wish list.

The café was quiet. A few people entered or left, but I quickly
became unaware of anyone except our group. Laura's dark eyes
focused on the face of her birth mother, watching the tears flow
over her cheeks as Jane translated Hyeja's words.

"I could not bear to see you dying!" The message was meant
for Laura in hopes that she would forgive a mother's inability to

save her child. The words were familiar. Laura had read them when she was ten years old and heard them again on Birth Mother's visit to Ohio.

I watched Laura on that sultry June day, six months into her away-from-home commitment, listening with her twenty-five years of wisdom to the words that her birth mother needed to repeat, to tell Laura again *why* she didn't raise her. Laura was old enough to look through the tears, into the eyes, and down into the heart of the woman who had birthed her.

This chat with Jane in the Seoul Café was different from the ones we had had with Aun in Ohio. This was more intimate. And this time Myeong-Suk was present. As he and Jane and Hyeja chatted back and forth, I felt regret that I could not understand one word of the conversation. I tried to pick up the tone of the words from Laura's expressions, for she understood some of what was being said. Her face was somber, sometimes with eyebrows pinched or eyes widened.

Jane translated, telling us "there had been conflict" between Laura's birth parents after Laura's heart problems had been identified. There had been intense conflict that lasted for weeks. They had disagreed about whether Laura should be placed for adoption or should stay with them in Korea. Even if the option of staying with them would mean she would die. "If SeonKyung is going to die, she will die with us," was Myeong-Suk's conviction. Hyeja fought back with, "If we have to give SeonKyung up to save her life, then we have to let her go."

In Korean culture, the husband is regarded as the sole source of authority. But Hyeja fought with all her strength to do what she believed was needed to save her daughter's life. Five months after their hearts had overflowed with joy at the birth of their twin daughters, Myeong-Suk and Hyeja signed papers of consent to place Laura for adoption.

We left the café with a different understanding of Laura's earliest months of life and a different awareness of her birth parents and their relationship. After a few moments of silence, Laura said, "Wow, I never knew how much my birth mother fought for me." Then she added, almost in a whisper, "She must have really loved me to do that."

The story of Laura's life before I knew her had been rewritten. As a mother, I viewed Hyeja differently than Laura viewed her. Understandably. Laura would get frustrated with her birth mother's need to see Laura and to talk with her. Laura had two mothers on opposite ends of the world, both with arms outstretched, reaching for her.

While walking home around 10 p.m. on her first day of teaching in Seoul, Laura had heard a woman's voice call out, "Roarra, Roarra!" It took several repeats of "Roarra" before she had realized that someone was calling out to *her*, giving the difficult-to-pronounce-in-Korean letter "L" the sound of the letter "R." It was her birth mother. Recognizing the woman running toward her, Laura's surprise was quickly bathed with annoyance. "She told me this was the first time she was able to walk me home from school," Laura recounted to me later. "She was *stalking* me! Can you *believe* that?"

Being shadowed home by her birth mother was more closeness than Laura could stomach. It disturbed Laura's need to keep her desired boundaries intact. I understood that about Laura—someone who needs her physical and personal space— but Hyeja did not.

Yet, when Laura told me the story, I couldn't help but be touched. *I* was Hyeja Kim. *I* was Birth Mother. And when I later reflected on Laura's stalking moment, I became the grieving *me* of decades before, driving around the block in our neighborhood, keeping an eye on a blond-headed boy walking to school, waiting for him to turn around, hoping that maybe—just maybe—he was *Shawn*. Not really hoping, but under grief's delusional power, *believing* for a moment that I was seeing *my* blond-headed boy.

When Laura had turned her head toward the voice calling her that night, Birth Mother's longing was fulfilled. When I had passed the blond-headed boy and he had turned his face toward me, my brief moment of living in a safe world where Shawn still lived disappeared.

Yet, as she rushed toward Laura along the brick-paved street in Seoul, Hyeja must have felt I was the lucky one. I was the mother who had walked Laura home from school. I had been the one to see so many of the beginnings, the firsts of my daughter's life, the life that another woman had delivered into the world. First lost tooth, first school concert, first spin on her two-wheeled bike, first notes on her violin, first no-touching-the-wall glide on her ice skates. Hyeja Kim's firstborn child had even navigated her first bow-legged, wobbly footsteps toward *my* outstretched arms.

Ten days had passed since our meeting in the café, and I clutched Laura's hand while dragging my wheeled carry-on luggage through the Incheon Airport. EunKyung navigated as Kevin and Birth Mother and Birth Father trailed behind. Kevin and I were flying home, leaving Laura to finish the seven remaining months of her teaching commitment.

Memories of the past three weeks in South Korea buzzed through my head. I was not ready to go home. Although Laura loved her teaching job and was settled and adjusted in her temporary home, I didn't want to leave without her.

We approached an escalator, its silver teeth folding into itself as it rotated down to our destination below. I hesitated.

"I can't go down that escalator," I said, tension and panic clinging to my voice. "Where's the elevator?"

As Laura looked at me, we heard a giggle from Hyeja. "Me, too, Kattee. Same, same." Then with her hands together, as if offering me something, Hyeja reached her arms out to me, then pulled them back and placed them on her own chest. She repeated, "Same, same."

"My birth mother is afraid of escalators too, Mom. Just like you." Hearing that news, I joined Laura and Hyeja in their laughter. "You and Birth Mother are *same, same*," Laura announced, grinning.

We pushed ourselves into the elevator, hit the down button, then exited near the security area. That was where we had to part.

Laura and I kissed and hugged and said our *I love yous*. I had hoped my tears would stay away, but they came anyway, spilling down my face. Birth Mother stood and watched. She saw our hugs, my tears.

"Same, same," I heard Birth Mother say again as I quickly turned away.

Yes, Hyeja and I. In more ways than not, we are *same, same*.

Intertwined

If you live to be a hundred, I want to live to be a hundred minus one day so I never have to live without you.

~ Winnie the Pooh

A few months after she returned home from South Korea, Laura and I decided to enroll together in an online creative nonfiction writing class at Columbus State Community College, the idea arising from our mutual interest and love of writing.

The class comprised twelve students of varying ages and backgrounds. "Write about being a mother," Laura advised. "You have so much you can say." She also saw my years of nursing as a source of shareable stories. But as anyone who has started to write nonfiction essays or memoir knows, and as Laura and I both discovered, the words that gestate in the head are not the same ones that emerge from the fingertips.

I started out writing about the impact of Shawn's death on my life and those of my family. I wrote about his life. I wrote about grief and joy. I told of the resulting lows in my life and the mountains I'd since climbed. I thought about my fears and had to find the courage to put them into words. And I struggled. Not with *keeping up*, because both Laura and I earned an A, but with *pulling up* those memories that were deep under layers of life's happenings. It was a painful yet beneficial struggle.

Laura wrote about her birth mother's visit to the United States and about her twin. She wrote about living in Korea, expanding on words first appearing in the blog daringly titled *Dodging Kim Jung-Il and other Misadventures in South Korea,* which she had kept while living in Seoul. Since our class was online, the others did not know Laura and I were related, although the professor may have suspected by the end of the semester, as our stories became strangely interwoven. Our professor provided just the right amount of mentoring and encouragement we needed, as both Laura and I enrolled in a "Writing to Publish" class the following semester.

Through writing, we relived and re-felt and remembered. We rediscovered ourselves and each other. Writing about our past led to talking more about our past. I had often avoided topics with Laura that revolved around her running-away years. Laura felt enough guilt and shame. I didn't want to inflict more. But now we were two adults. Through sharing our writing with each other, we drifted with caution toward those often-fiery times a decade and more in the past. One day I asked, just being curious, "How did you decide on the yin-yang for your tattoo? Is that something you had been wanting?"

"Got it out of a book the tattoo artist had of designs for people who didn't know what they wanted. Which I didn't," Laura admitted about her sixteen-year-old self, "because I didn't *plan* to get one. We just walked by the tattoo shop and decided to go in and look through the book." The "we" Laura referred to consisted of her and the guy (whom I mistakenly had believed was a college student) who had befriended her when she was on the lam, providing her with a place to stay.

"We decided we wanted to get yin-yang symbols because we liked the one we saw and thought it would be cute to have matching tattoos." Then she casually added, "He didn't even know my real name. I gave him an alias."

Laura had told him her name was Arani. She chose it because it was her spiritual or Sanskrit name, a fire sign meaning sun.

Similar to SeonKyung, sometimes spelled SunKyung. Meaning to be bright, like the sun.

Hearing the story of Laura's now almost-fifteen-year-old yin-yang tattoo made me laugh. Since I first saw it, I had assumed it had great significance to her, but in reality, she had acquired it on a whim. I could pinpoint on the calendar the exact date she got it, even though I was not there. I doubt Laura could do the same.

The yin-yang that rests above Laura's heart tells the story of a young girl who happened to wander into a tattoo shop while running away from her permanent home. She obtained a permanent tattoo while in a temporary relationship with a temporary name that had the same meaning as the name given to her at birth by her temporary parents who later placed her for adoption. The day after this young girl chose the tattoo, she was found by the efforts of her permanent adoptive mother who had been running toward her, trying to track her down.

I am the mother Laura needed. I am the mother who, having lost a child, had the strength and the audacity to do whatever I could possibly do to help bring my missing child home. To never give up on her. Laura is the daughter I needed. Seeing life through her eyes softened the pain of loss for me. Seeing life through her eyes gave me hope and resiliency and immense joy.

I have grown to cherish the beauty in the yin-yang that decorates Laura's chest, resting on her breastbone above her heart. I view it as representing *us*. Laura and me.

Two complementary and intertwined energies blended together.

ACKNOWLEDGMENTS

Thank you, Dear Reader, for holding my book in your hands and reading the words that have been in my heart. I hope you have smiled or laughed or cried as you read. And if you too have experienced any sadness or anxiety in your lifetime, or have lived through the death of your child, I especially wish that my words have given you comfort and hope.

I am grateful for my writing community. For Kate Hopper, my mentor, editor, and overall cheerleader extraordinaire who gave me the gift of believing in me from the moment she first read my words. For all my MFA faculty mentors at Ashland University in Ashland, Ohio: Bonnie J. Rough, Robert Root, Steven Harvey, Thomas Larson, Daniel Lehman, and Leila Philip. Thank you to my Ashland Summer Residency suitemates Jan Shoemaker, who guided me through my first summer program, and Joy Gaines-Friedler, who shared the second and third summers with me and instilled in me a greater love of poetry.

Thank you to all my classmates, friends, and fellow lovers of words who read my beginnings and drafts. And a big thank you and deepest gratitude to the readers and blurbers of my final manuscript: Christine Bowers, Jeanne Clement, Steven Harvey, Kate Hopper, Shannon Johnson, Thomas Larson, and Lee Martin.

I am grateful to the team at KiCam Projects, most especially to Jennifer Scroggins, who patiently guides me when I'm lost and confused, and to Mark Sullivan for his beautiful cover and book design..

In June, as I was working feverishly on edits and changes to chapter ten, I called Dick (Dr. Richard Stranges). His is the only name of the treating physicians discussed in my book that I did not change. We talked about a few mutual patients, his needing to complete a class for his continued certification, but mostly about our families. The following weekend, I struggled through the final changes on that challenging chapter and sent it on its way to KiCam Projects on Monday. On Tuesday afternoon, I received a phone call from Dick's grandson. "Papa's gone," was his message. And just like that, Dick had passed beyond that "mystic veil." I am immensely grateful that our paths crossed and that our relationship spanned decades. I am grateful for the gift of his kindness to my children, for the wisdom he shared with me, and for always making me feel that I was a very unique and important person in this world.

I'm grateful I have a family to love and that they love me. To Pete and Ryan and Elizabeth and their spouses for understanding my drive to tell my story. Thank you to my granddaughter, Mary, for sharing my love of writing and for being curious and brave enough to read an early draft.

And so much love and gratitude to my dear husband, Kevin, who besides being the best proofreader in the universe, has the ability to still love and support me when I'm at my temperamentally, obsessively, artistically worst that I could possibly be.

And then there's Laura. "It's *your* story, Mom," she repeatedly tells me when I question the content of my writing. "It's *your* story to tell." Thank you, Dear Laura, for being the heart of my story. For your smiles, your laughter, and your love. For being my daughter and my best friend.

ABOUT THE AUTHOR
Kathleen English Cadmus is a mental health nurse practitioner who earned her MFA in Creative Writing from Ashland (Ohio) University. As a bereaved parent of a son and an adoptive parent of a daughter with bipolar disorder, Kathleen has been active in both the adoption communities and the mental health arenas. She has had her writing published in local newspapers, adoption newsletters, and the nursing anthology *Learning to Heal* (Kent State University Press, 2018). Kathleen lives in Worthington, Ohio, with her husband, Kevin, and is a mother to five children and grandmother to seven.